Here's what people are saying abo
The Story of Ancient Greek Women Athletes.

"Well written with well documented research, which shows the truth of women's role in ancient Greek society. The book, by placing things in their proper perspective, gives another picture of women's role in ancient society and consequently, a new picture of that ancient society itself."

Archeology Magazine of Greece

"Congratulations on a wonderful book. Your book gives a complete picture of the games in ancient Greece, with invaluable information on women's contributions in ancient sports, which had been overlooked and forgotten."

Professor Stylianos Alexiou, Archeologist, former Director of the Heraklion Museum, Krete

"The remarkable research of Anne Reese and Irini Vallera-Rickerson brings to the surface women's activities in the field of athletics in ancient Greece."

Katerina P. Panagopoulou, Ambassador of Greece for Sports, Tolerance, and Fair Play to the Council of Europe

"I studied your wonderful book carefully and found it extremely exciting. It is written in a clear manner supported by scholarly documentation. The study of women in ancient Greek sports was very much needed as it brings into focus women's contributions to the ancient world of sports. This book eliminates the myth of the non-existence of women in athletics in ancient times. It proves through ancient texts, inscriptions, and art that the existence of women athletes goes back at least as far as the Minoan Civilization. Congratulations on a fantastic book."

Anna Tziropoulou-Efstathiou, Member of the Greek Academy at Bilbao, Spain

*Cover Photo of Statue*

Greek 6th century B.C. mirror handle in the form of a female figure standing on recumbent lion. The figure is holding what seems to be an oil flask in the hand at her side, which was used to oil the athlete's body. This, along with her muscular appearance, suggests this is a woman athlete. Bronze, height 13-5/8 inch: "The Metropolitan Museum of Art, Fletcher Fund, 1938. (38.11.3) All rights reserved, The Metropolitan Museum of Art."

# ATHLETRIES
## The Untold History of Ancient Greek Women Athletes

(Athletries is the Greek
word for women athletes)

ANNE C. REESE

IRINI VALLERA-RICKERSON

NIGHTOWL PUBLICATIONS
Costa Mesa, California  92627-9998, U..S.A.

ATHLETRIES
The Untold History of Ancient
Greek Women Athletes

Copyright © 2002
By Nightowl Publications

Published in Greece by IDEOTHEATRO,
under the title:
*Ancient Greek Women Athletes.*

| Written by: | Anne C. Reese |
| | Irini Vallera-Rickerson |
| Edited by | Kathy Bryant |
| Illustrated by | Jeff Kern |
| Cover Design by | Phil Patterson |
| Design by | Mylo Productions |

All rights reserved.
No part of this book may be reproduced or transmitted
in any form without written permission from the publisher,
except by a reviewer who may quote brief passages for review purposes.

Library of Congress Catalog Number: 2002101871
ISBN: 0-9714984-0-7
First Printing, 2002

Nightowl Publications
P.O. Box 10755
Costa Mesa, CA 92627-9998

www.Nightowlpublications.com

Printed in The United States of America

This book is dedicated
to our parents:

Dorothy and David Reese
Lena and Vasily Valleras

# ACKNOWLEDGMENTS

We would like to thank all those who made this book possible, in particular:

Stylianos Alexiou, archeologist, former Director of the Herakleion Archeological
Museum, Krete.
Jenny Beach, graduate student, assistant in the Thesaurus Linguae Gracae program
at the University of California at Irvine.
Mortimer Chambers, professor in the Department of History at the University of
California at Los Angeles.
Stephen G. Miller, archeologist, professor in the Department of Classics at the
University of California at Berkley, and Director of Excavations at Nemea.
Nick Nicholas, PhD, in the Thesaurus Linguae Gracae program at the University of
California at Irvine.
Maria C. Pantelia, Director of the Thesaurus Linguae Gracae program at the
University of California at Irvine.
Nikolaos Yalouris, archeologist, former General Inspector of Antiquities of Greece.

We also thank:

Mr. Dasios, archeologist at the Archeological Museum of Delphi.
Eva Gramatikaki, archeologist at the Herakleion Archeological Museum, Krete.
John Haddick, Advanced Publishing Consultants Inc., Santa Ana, California.
The staff at the Kerameikos Museum, Athens.
Adonis Kiros, Estia Newspaper, Athens.
Maria Korma, scholar, Athens.
Demetrios Limberopoulos, Benakion Library, Athens.
Ted Nuce, World Champion bull-rider.
The staff at the Orange Coast College Library, Costa Mesa, California, in particular
Joanna Brand, Carl Morgan and Edith Riestra.
Thanos Papathanasopoulos, architect/archeologist, Athens.
Thomas F. Scanlon, professor in the department of Classics at the University of
California at Riverside.
Julia Sutton, digital artist
Dorothy J. Thompson, professor at the University of Cambridge, England.
Daphne Vallera, professor, Athens.
Lena Vallera, scholar, Athens.
Olympia Vikatou, archeologist, Archeological Museum, Olympia.
Wayne Wilson, Director of Amateur Athletic foundation, Los Angeles, California.

# TABLE OF CONTENTS

## CHAPTER FOUR: THE PYTHIAN GAMES

## CHAPTER FIVE: THE NEMEAN GAMES

## CHAPTER SIX: THE ISTHMIAN GAMES

## CHAPTER SEVEN: THE STATUS OF WOMEN
## IN ANCIENT GREECE

## CHAPTER EIGHT: FESTIVALS

## CHAPTER NINE: THE MODERN DAY OLYMPICS

# INTRODUCTION

The legendary prowess of ancient Greek male athletes has been written about in odes, poems and stories down through the ages. From the same ancient sources that give us the names of these male athletes we also find the names of female athletes who competed and were honored for their victories. Why has it taken so long for history to recognize the achievements of these female athletes? The answer lies in today.

We are now living in an age when women are questioning their roles in all areas of life. Women are daily breaking through the barriers that have kept them from living lives to their fullest potential. In doing this, they are looking not only to the future, but to the past for the recognition and inspiration from those women who came before and achieved their own potential during times even more difficult for women than today.

One area in which women have been making tremendous strides in the past twenty-five years is in the field of sports. Women now have the opportunity to participate in sports for the same reasons that men have always been able to participate. These reasons are as varied as better physical health, a professional athletic career, or just for enjoyment. Today most societies promote the participation of women in athletic contests, the epitome being the Olympic Games. There are now professional women's sports' teams in basketball, volleyball and baseball, among others.

In the past, women have been viewed as inferior to men, which has resulted in a lack of information on their contributions to society. The roles of women have been narrowly depicted as that of mothers, sisters and wives of men. Society has been led to believe that prior to the last half of the twentieth century women had not taken an active role in sports. Therefore, it is not surprising that it is almost unknown today, except in academic circles, that the women of ancient Greece participated in the various athletic contests taking place throughout Greece.

The Western world has always been interested in ancient Greece. This interest greatly increased during the Renaissance in the fifteenth century and continued with the Neoclassical movement in the eighteenth and nineteenth centuries, reaching its peak in the nineteenth century Victorian Era. The Neoclassical movement was the result of ongoing excavations at Pompeii; the archeological discovery of Herculaneum (Erolano); and the writings of the eighteenth century archeologist, Johann Joachim Winckelmann.

Pompeii and Herculaneum were two ancient Roman cities located on the Bay of Naples, Italy. Both towns were destroyed by the volcanic eruption of Mt. Vesuvius, in 79 A.D., thus preserving excellent examples of their ancient lifestyles. Archeological excavations of the two cities, in the eighteenth century, stimulated interest in the ancient world. Johann Winckelmann published his book, "History of Ancient Art," that delved into the arts and ideas which produced the art of ancient Greece and Rome. His book greatly influenced the art, decorative arts, architecture, and many other areas of eighteenth century life.

During the Victorian Era (1833–1901) interest in ancient Greece reached its peak and numerous publications were written based on ancient Greek sources and archeological discoveries. The lack of information on ancient women in these publications is due to the Victorian mentality regarding women. This mentality was one in which women were viewed as inferior to men; therefore, their contributions were not worth mentioning. Any information found in ancient texts relating to women in sports would especially be ignored since sports were considered inappropriate activities for women.

The people of the Victorian Era are notorious for their limited view of women. The typical attitude was expressed by Baron Pierre de Coubertin, who

Figure 1 – Victorian women doing the only exercise thought suitable for them by Victorian society, applauding male endeavors.

renewed the Olympic Games in 1896, when he defined the Olympic Games as, *"…the solemn and periodic exhaltation of male athleticism with internationalism as a base, loyalty as a means, art for its setting, and female applause as reward."*[1] It seems the only athletic ability women should possess was being able to put two hands together to applaud male endeavors. (figure 1)

Even if Coubertin and his contemporaries had realized that women had been participating in ancient Greek athletics, at least as early as 1900 B.C., it would not have mattered. Their prejudices against women doing anything that had them "perspiring in public"[2] or assuming "ungainly positions"[3] permeated their society. The result of this attitude was books written during this time ignored ancient women and their contributions in anything other than a domestic activity.

Most of the books written during the first half of the twentieth century were based on books written during the Victorian Era, that ignored the ancient sources and, thus, perpetuated the lack of documentation on women's contributions.

3

Our intent in writing this book is to recognize ancient women as much more than relations of men. We have tried to do this by focusing on an area of life that has been dominated by men. By documenting women's participation in the ancient Greek world of sports, through athletic games and festivals, we hope to give one more piece of the puzzle to reconstruct the total picture of women in history as capable, independent thinkers, and valuable contributors to society.

Participation in sports was not unique to only a few women, in a local area, over a short period of time, but seemed to involve many women coming to the games from all areas of Ancient Greece, and extending over a period of hundreds of years.

Information is meager on ancient Greek women athletes. The fact that we have identified any women winners, indicates there must have been many other women in the competitions who did not win, were not commemorated, and therefore, were forgotten. Even those who did win did not always have a lasting monument. Women at Olympia were allowed to honor themselves with their names engraved on statues,[4] which were put in the Temple of Hera. Several statuettes of girl runners have been found and archeologists believe that these were probably made to honor the winners in an ancient Greek game or festival.

This book is based on ancient sources, such as, ancient texts, inscriptions, art and artifacts. We have relied heavily on Pausanias' accounts of his travels through ancient Greece. Pausanias lived during the second century A.D., and wrote what could be considered the first travel guide in his books called Descriptions of Greece. These accounts of Greece are recorded in ten books and are the major source on ancient Greek sports. Pausanias gives first-hand information on women runners who were his contemporaries. He describes inscriptions on statues and monuments still in existence during his time, dedicated to the women who won at various athletic contests that took place hundreds of years earlier. Archeological discoveries in modern times have confirmed the general accuracy of Pausanias' writings.

Pausanias recorded the stories, that had become tradition, relating deeds of ancient Greek women athletes. Through the centuries the truth in these stories has been elaborated and exaggerated to the point that, today, they have been classified as myths. Also, most of the stories were recorded long after the actual event and have no provable, historical documentation.

The theory of the Greek scholar, Euhemeros, who lived at the end of the third century B.C., was that all myths were based on historical facts and it was the job of the scholar to sift through layers of fiction to find the facts. Euhemeros' theory has been found to be true in a number of cases. Archeological discoveries have produced evidence bringing some myths into the realm of fact.

The ancient city of Troy, mentioned in the eighth century B.C. epic poem called *The Iliad*, by Homer, was long thought to be a myth until it was proven to be fact, and unearthed by German amateur archeologist Heinrich Schliemann, in the nineteenth century.

The Palace of Nestor in Pylos, also thought to have been mythological, was discovered by a joint Greek-American effort led by Carl W. Blegan and K. Kourouniotes, in 1939. The Palace of King Minos, once considered a myth, was discovered on Krete by British archeologist Sir Arthur Evans, in the early 1900's.

Of course, this does not mean that all myths are based in fact. We, the authors, tend to believe that most myths did begin with actual people doing extraordinary deeds, or with events that had significant affects on the lives of the people of the time.

The benefit of being turned into a myth is it becomes such an entertaining story that a tradition is created, thereby, keeping the people and events alive for future generations. Then, these future generations are given the opportunity to determine what are the seeds of truth in the myth. These seeds of truth give us clues to our ancient past. Allowing that many myths can have some basis in truth, it is up to each individual to accept or reject what they believe this truth to be.

A brief history of ancient Greece is given to allow the reader a context in which to place the games and festivals. Dates given are approximations, since exact dates for the ancient world are continually debated by scholars.

When information is used from inscriptions of women winners in games or festivals, we have recorded it exactly as it was written in ancient Greek. The ancient Greek is then translated into modern Greek and English.

Sometimes the woman's name, the game, and the event in which she won are the only pieces of information available. Often there are only one or two pieces of the above information available. In almost all cases there is no further information on these women. Just listing their names would not do justice to their courage and determination to participate in a male-dominated field. Therefore, to help the reader relate to the person behind the name, and for their enjoyment, we have taken the liberty to write short scenarios on some of the women winners. Information for the scenarios is taken from ancient sources. Only the women's emotions and daily routines are added from our imaginations.

The scenarios were written with the belief that human emotions have remained basically the same from ancient times to present. The impetuses eliciting these emotions, such as athletic contests, have also remained the same.

We still get excited and cheer for our favorite team. We encourage our children to take part in school sports and express our pride and joy when they win. We raise the funds to send our best athletes to local, national, and international games and have ceremonies in which they are presented with trophies. We love and respect our athletes.

Was it really so much different in ancient Greece? Information from ancient sources tells us no. Athletes were honored and emulated. They were given prizes and statues were created to depict their feats. Some were professional athletes who competed in many different games. It requires very little effort to imagine the feelings of the ancients as they attended the athletic events of their day and cheered their favorite athletes on to victory.

To realize that the ancient tradition of athletic competition involved the participation of women opens a whole new perspective in our approach to history. We now know that women played an important and active role in areas previously thought open to men only.

Every woman who has ever risked crossing the line, whether it has been the finishing line in sports or the imaginary line that tell us certain jobs or activities are "men only," has laid a stepping stone toward the goal of equality for all people.

FOOTNOTES: Introduction

1.      Coubertin, 1912 Essay, Leigh, 1974.
2.      Ibid.
3.      Ibid.
4.      Pausanias, BK. V.XVI.3,4.

Ancient Greece: Cities

Greece: Regions

# BRIEF HISTORY

The island of Krete, which is located in the Mediterranean Sea about 240 kilometers south of Athens, is a good starting place to gain an understanding of the history of ancient Greece.

Remains of a Neolithic culture, dating from the sixth to the end of the third millennium B.C., were discovered on Krete. The people of this ancient culture domesticated animals, farmed the land, made decorated pottery, and knew how to use stone for building houses. Female figurines were discovered implying that they worshipped a fertility goddess.

At the end of the third millennium a Bronze Age culture, known as the Minoan Civilization, began to emerge. The Minoans took advantage of the island's natural assets. Surrounded by water, they took to the sea, which they dominated through their skill as seafarers. They opened shipping routes for trade to three continents: Europe, Asia, and Africa. Fertile soil and a mild climate promoted agriculture. The Minoans created a peaceful, prosperous, and sophisticated civilization advanced in the arts, architecture, and engineering. This great civilization lasted over 1500 years reaching its peak in the eighteenth to the sixteenth centuries B.C.

The Minoan civilization is believed to have ended around 1450 B.C. It is not known what brought about the end of this great civilization. The Minoan King Minos, his people, and his palace at Knossos became a myth, which was passed down in epic poems and stories through the ages.

Homer, who was an eighth century B.C. poet, stated that Minoan Krete was heavily populated with more than ninety cities.[1] Today, archeologists have uncovered numerous ancient, palace complexes attesting to the veracity of Homer's work.

Sir Arthur Evans, a British archeologist, started excavating the palace at Knossos, Krete, in 1900. He uncovered a highly developed civilization. Evans believed the Minoans worshipped a Mother Goddess and that they had a matriarchal society.

Towards the end of the Minoan civilization, the Bronze Age culture of the Mycenaeans was developing in the area of the Peloponnese, on the Greek mainland. The Mycenaean civilization, also known as the Helladic civilization, lasted from approximately 1580 – 1100 B.C. The civilization is named after the most important cultural and political center of the time, Mycenae.

Mycenae was discovered in 1876 by the same German archeologist who discovered Troy, Heinrich Schliemann. Schliemann uncovered five royal grave sites known as the Shaft Graves. The rich contents of these graves started the study of the Greek Bronze Age on the mainland.

The Mycenaeans gained control of the sea after the Minoan civilization was destroyed. Mycenaean centers were composed of small, independent townships centered around fortified palaces, which became powerful empires. These empires were ruled by kings. Two of the main dieties worshipped were Gaia, representing mother earth, and the Goddess Hera. They also worshipped numerous other goddesses and gods.

The declining wealth and power of the Mycenaean empires started around 1300 B.C. The Dorians, who were from the northwestern part of the Greek mainland, invaded and destroyed the last of the Mycenaean civilization about 1100 B.C.

The "Dark Ages" in Greece came with the Dorian invasion. They lasted until circa 800 B.C. With the Dorians came the Iron Age and the extinction of the Bronze Age. Little is known of the Dorian Era. There are a few remains, but not enough to get a clear picture of this period.

Hellenic Greece came into existence around 800 B.C. and ended with the death of Alexander the Great in 323 B.C. Palace centers from the Mycenaean period, that survived the Dorian invasion, evolved into independent communities called city-states by the eighth century B.C. These city-states were not politically united and often quarreled with each other. However, they were united by a common language and religion.

Three of the most famous city-states were Athens, Sparta, and Korinth. Due to an expanding population with too little farmable land to support it, colonization of other lands began. This mainly occurred in Sicily and southern Italy. These colonies were known as Magna Graecia, which means Greater Greece in Latin. Colonization contributed to the spread of Greek ideas.

By the seventh century B.C., there were several forms of government that ruled the city-states. The most important of these were the democratic, oligarchic, and tyrannic. Their religious beliefs were based on numerous goddesses and gods, which were believed to be immortal, super beings with human traits. Hera became the main goddess and Zeus was the main god.

Games and festivals, which most likely originated from earlier religious practices, gained in popularity. Women, as well as men, were competing. The first time that names of winners were recorded in the Olympic Games was in 776 B.C.

Around the fifth century B.C. Persia invaded mainland Greece twice over a ten year period. The Persians were defeated in their first invasion by the Athenians at the Battle of Marathon in 490 B.C. When the Persians tried to invade a second time the Greeks, unified for the first time, defeated the Persians in a navel battle at the Straight of Salamis in 480 B.C., and at Plataea in 479 B.C. The Greek defeat of the Persians changed world history. If the Persians had won the culture of the today's Western world might be based on the Persian culture instead of the Greek one.

After many of the city-states unified under the Athenian governor

Perikles to defeat the Persians, Athens became the cultural Mecca of the known world. This period is known as the Golden Age of Greece, 461–431 B.C., and it was during this time the Greeks produced their greatest arts.

Sparta defeated Athens in the Peloponnesian War, 431–404 B.C. Philip II of Macedonia in 338 B.C., unified the city-states of Greece that had once again become disunited. In 336 B.C. Philip's son, Alexander the Great, became ruler and began his campaign to conquer the known world. Greece acquired vast territories under Alexander. When Alexander the Great died in 323 B.C. the Hellenistic Age began.

During the Hellenistic Age, 323–330 B.C., Greek ideas and culture were spread throughout Egypt, the Near East, and as far east as Punjab, India. Egypt had Greek rulers on the throne for almost 300 years from the line of Ptolemies. Kleopatra VII was of Greek decent, and inherited the Egyptian throne from her father, Ptolemy XI in 51 B.C. She was the last of the Greek rulers to sit on the Egyptian throne. The Hellenistic period was a time of great strides in science, art, and education. Many people worshipped the gods of Egypt, while others continued to worship the ancient Greek goddesses and gods.

Greece became a Roman colony in 146 B.C. and the Greek colony of Egypt came under Roman rule in 30 B.C., after the sea battle at Aktio, when the ships of Kleopatra and Anthony were defeated by the Roman ships. Greece experienced 300 years of unbroken peace under the Romans.

FOOTNOTES: Brief History

1.      *The Toils and Travels of Odysseus,* translated by C.A. Pease, published by Allyn and  Bacon, U.S.A., 1926, "Odysseus Talks with Penelope," XV. 20.

# CHAPTER ONE

## SPORTS IN THE AEGEAN

The Aegean Civilization, 3000-1100 B.C., consisted of four main cultures which were located on the islands and shores of the Aegean Sea. These cultures were: the Minoan culture, on the island of Krete; the Mycenaean (Helladic) culture, on the Greek mainland; the Cycladic culture, on a group of islands north of Krete; and the Troadic culture, in the ancient city of Troy and its surrounding area; as well as, the Hellespont, now called the Dardanelles in Turkey.

So far, evidence for women in sports during the Aegean civilization has been found in two of the above cultures: the Minoan, which was the first important civilization in Europe; and the Mycenaean. The end of the Minoan civilization and the beginning of the Mycenaean overlapped for approximately 250 years, and a strong Minoan influence was felt on the mainland.

Documented evidence of women in sports dates back to the middle of the Minoan civilization. Sir Arthur Evans, a British archeologist, was mainly responsible for the excavations at Knossos on Krete, which brought to light information on the Minoan Civilization, 3000 to 1450 B.C. (figure 2) Evans gives a detailed account of his excavations in four volumes called, *The Palace of Minos at Knossos*, written in 1930.[1] The site of Knossos and Evans' books have become the major source of information on Minoan society.

The Minoans developed a sophisticated Bronze Age culture. They were skilled seafarers, which allowed them to develop trade on an international level. Thukydides, an ancient Greek historian from the fifth century B.C., writes *"...he (King Minos) was the first man to hold sway over the Aegean with his fleet."*[2] They built huge palaces requiring a high degree of architectural skill, and were advanced in the arts. Information on Minoan society can be seen through their art.

Minoan art such as fresco fragments, clay seals, and reliefs found at Knossos give archeological evidence on sports popular during the Minoan period. Bull-jumping and bull-wrestling[3] were popular and women, as well as men, performed these amazing feats. Bull sports were probably religious in nature, which is suggested by the "Sacral Knot" (figure 3) found in some of the artwork showing these games.[4] They were probably performed to honor the Minoan's main deity, the Mother Goddess. (figure 4) The bull, apparently, represents a fertility god worshipped along with her.[5] Evans thought bull-wrestling may have been practiced as far back as 1900 B.C., at the beginning of the Minoan palace periods. He based his belief on the evidence found at Knossos in the

Figure 2 - Sir Arthur Evans on site at Knossos.

form of painted reliefs on the porticoes above the Northern Entrance Passage. In the reliefs both women and men are depicted "herding and catching"[6] cattle in the open country. Evans called these "country sports,"[7] because of the

Figure 3 - Sacral knot.

background scenes on the reliefs portraying the rocky ground and trees of the country. He felt they were representative of the early, ceremonial version of the sport, which later became a more structured, religious performance practiced in bull-rings near the palaces.[8]

Bull-wrestling was also a popular sport in the Mycenaean culture. Two ancient, gold cups known as "Vapheio Cup A and B," from circa 1500 B.C., show bull-wrestling. The cups were found in a gravesite at Vapheio, located on the Peloponnese. "Vapheio Cup A" depicts the figure of a girl with her legs and arms locked around a bull's horns in such a way that the bull cannot gore her. (figure 5) The girl has twisted the bull's head to the point where the bull will either fall to the ground or his neck will be broken.[9]

Evans determined the figure on "Vapheio Cup A" was that of a girl due to the short curls of hair fringing her forehead, with the rest of her long hair bound in a coil at the back of her neck to prevent it from becoming a hindrance. This hairstyle is indicative of a female in Minoan iconography. The Vapheio Cup was either made by the Minoans and found its way to the Mycenaean mainland or the design was of Minoan influence. On the cup the only feature that distinguishes the girl from the boy is her hairstyle.

A number of the fresco fragments found at Knossos and dated by Evans to be from the First Late Minoan phase (eighteenth to the fifteenth century B.C.,)[10] depict bull-jumping and are known as the "Toreador Frescoes." Evans suggests that bull-jumping, like a circus act, was performed by women and men who were highly trained acrobats with bulls that were carefully raised and trained as well.

The "Toreador Frescoes" show both women and men with straps bound

Figure 4 – Drawing of the ancient "Mother Goddess" of the Minoans.

around their hands and wrists, most likely to support the wrists and to allow a better grip on the bull. There are several ways to distinguish women from men in Minoan iconography. The most obvious is skin color. Women are depicted with white skin and men with skin of a brownish red hue. Another distinctive feature is women are shown with short, symmetrical curls over their foreheads and temples, sometimes with brightly colored bands around their brow. Their loin-cloths are the same as the men's but with more design and color variation.

The most well known of the "Toreador Frescoes" is called "Bull-leaping," and shows two women and one man bull-jumping. (figure 6) It has been possible to restore the entire composition of the "Bull-leaping" fresco. This fresco portrays a man in the act of jumping over the bull's back and dismounting in a backward somersault over the rear of the bull, where a woman waits to help him dismount. The next jumper is a woman who is in the process of grabbing the horns of the onrushing bull in order to do her leap.

There are various theories on how bull-jumping was accomplished, all equally dangerous. A drawing made for Sir Arthur Evans by Theodore Fyfe, represents one way bull-jumping may have been performed. (figure 7) The position of female acrobat number one is based on the acrobat grasping the bull's horns depicted in the "Bull-leaping" fresco. (figure 6) In the diagram, a female acrobat grabs the horns from the front of the onrushing bull; when the bull throws his head back she is catapulted onto his back, in this case, into a standing position. She then dismounts over the bull's rear. Evans writes that the first part of the stunt, as shown, was found to be humanly impossible to perform; however, the remainder of the cycle is a possible theory.

Imagine 2,000 pounds of bull with sharp pointed horns charging directly at you. You're not supposed to run but, instead, interact with this ton of muscle and to look good, with your beautiful jewelry and hair curled, at the same time. It's enough to "curl your hair!"

The opinion of a veteran "steer-wrestler," who was consulted during Evans' time, was that grabbing the horns of an onrushing bull in order to start a somersault was an impossible feat. A person would not be able to keep his or her balance to perform because a charging bull moves his head to the side to gore anyone in his way.[11]

In 1998 world champion bull-rider, Ted Nuce, from Oakdale, California, was consulted about bull-leaping and the possibility of people performing the feats depicted in the frescoes found at Knossos. Nuce said that anything was possible if the women and men were acrobats and if the bull were highly trained. He said that bulls could be trained to allow acrobats to perform almost any stunt they wanted with the bull. Nuce went on to say he had a

Figure 5 - Line drawing of "Vapheio Cup A," depicting the figure of a girl with her legs and arms locked around a bull's horns. The cup is located in the Archeological Museum, Athens.

friend who taught his bull to lie down and roll over so that he could pet his stomach. Ted Nuce's information corroborates the veracity of the scenes depicted of life in Minoan society on frescoes found at Knossos.

A fragment of a fresco, from the scene of a bull-ring, shows a girl in the act of leaping onto, or off of, a bull. (figure 8)  The Kretan Government gave this fragment, among others, to Sir Arthur Evans, and it is now in the Ashmolean Museum in Oxford, England.

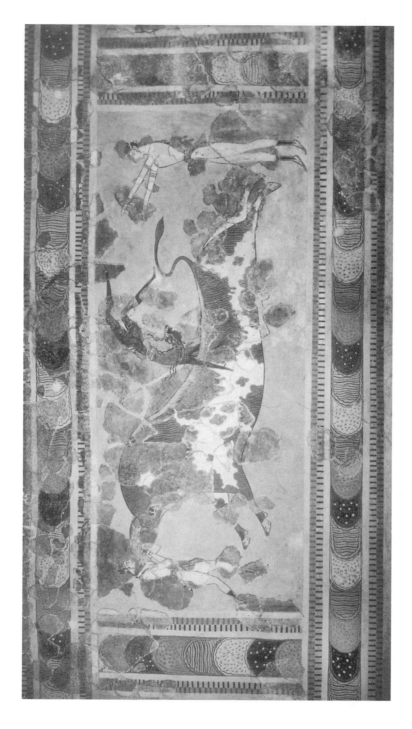

Figure 6 – "Bull-leaping" from the "Toreador frescoes." Fresco shows two women and a man bull-jumping. Archeological Museum, Herakleion, Krete.

Clay seals (see page 27) found at Knossos give an idea of the different methods of performing bull-jumping. (figure 9a,b,c,d,e)  We know that both women and men participated in bull-jumping; therefore, it is not important to distinguish the sex of the figures, which cannot be determined on most of the seals. Evans does say the standing figure on the seal shown in figure 9a is intended to be a girl; he does not explain how this was determined.

A gold signet ring was found depicting another form of bull-jumping. The jumper is shown doing a back-flip to dismount over the bull's rump. (figure 10)

Due to the beautiful jewelry, carefully curled hair, and colorful decorations shown on the girls bull-jumping, Evans believed they were from the

Figure 7 - Drawing based on drawing by Theodore Fyfe, showing one way bull-jumping may have been performed.

upper classes of Minoan society. He believed women held a more prominent position in Minoan society than men. This was shown in Minoan frescoes and their worship of the Mother Goddess. The panel entitled the "Grand Stand" from the frescoes called the "Miniature Frescoes," depicts women sitting in all the front seats of the grand stands and mingling freely with the men. (figure 11)

Various books and articles written today state women in Minoan society participated in other sports such as running, swimming, and hunting. They cite as evidence for women running Hogarth's seal showing three figures wearing skirts with their arms bent at the elbow as if in a running position. According to archeologist Alexiou Stylianos, a leading authority on the Minoan civilization and former head of the Herakleion Museum on Krete, these figures are not running but walking while performing a religious ceremony. The skirts they are wearing were of leather and were worn by either women or men, since both sexes performed the ceremony.

Unless we use the depictions of what archeologist call goddesses doing sports activities, such as hunting, there is currently not any evidence to support female sporting activities other than those of the bull sports. However, it is likely that women during the Minoan and Mycenaean civilizations did swim, run, and hunt.

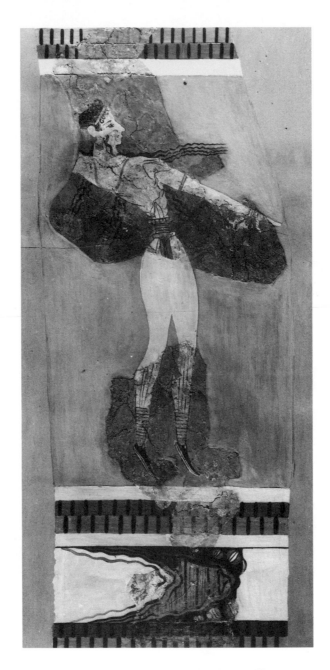

Figure 8 – Fresco fragment showing a girl in the act of leaping onto,
or off of, a bull. Ashmolean Museum, Oxford, England.

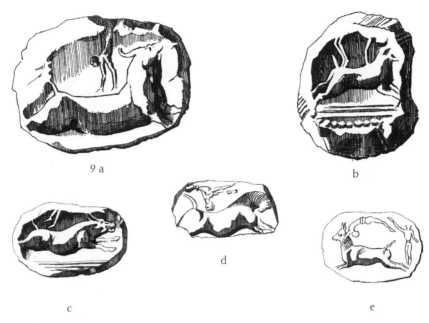

9 a                                                        b

d

c                                                        e

Figures 9a, b, c, d, e – Seals depicting various methods of how bull-jumping may have been
performed. Archeological Museum, Herakleion, Krete.

Figure 10 – Gold signet ring with a depiction of a form of bull-jumping.
Ashmolean Museum, Oxford, England.

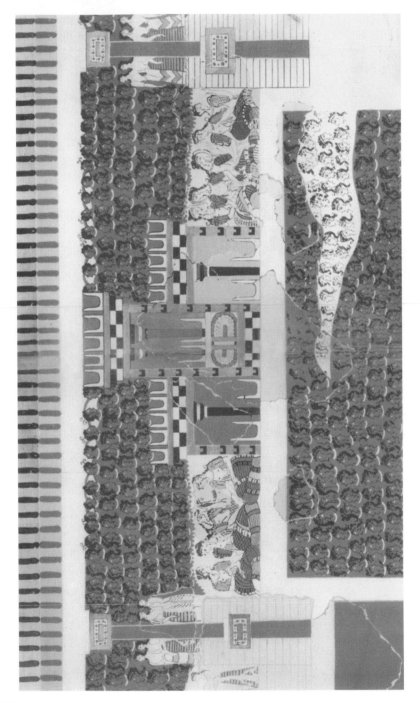

Figure 11 – "Grand Stand Fresco" showing women, who are depicted in white, seated in the front rows of the grand stand and mixing freely with men. Archeological Museum, Herakleion, Krete.

## WHAT ARE FRESCOES?

A fresco refers to a painting where pigments are applied to a plaster surface. There are two types of frescoes, the *buon fresco* and the *fresco secco*. The technique used by the artist in making the fresco determines the type of fresco. To create a *buon fresco* the artist applies pigment to a wet plaster surface and the color soaks into and becomes part of the wall. *Fresco secco* is where the artist uses the technique of applying the pigment, which is mixed with an organic preservative such as egg whites, to a dry surface. Often, both methods were used on the same fresco; after the *buon fresco* was dry additional paint was added to depict details.

Hundreds of sea pebbles have been found that were used as tools to smooth the wet plaster walls before the color was applied. The surface to be painted was first outlined by stretching a string across it to leave an impression. The figures, and sometimes the details, were also outlined by using this "taut string" method or by using a tool to make the incisions. Now the artist was ready to apply the colors.

The pigments used for the colors in the frescoes were obtained from minerals. The three main colors used were blue, ochre, and red. Lime water was used to dilute these colors to get various shades. Also, other colors were created by mixing black with blue for light gray and black with red for brown. White from plaster was added to red for a pink shade.

Most of the frescoes found in Akrotiri were pieced together from walls that had collapsed. When the plaster fragments of a fresco are found the archeologist calls in a conservator whose job is to remove the fragments to the laboratory for restoration, which is an intricate and time consuming process. Piecing together some of the frescoes is like working on a very complicated jigsaw puzzle.

## WHAT ARE SEALS?

Seals refer to small carved or engraved objects made of a hard material, usually stone, bone, or hardened clay. They were used to make an impression on clay or wax, which denoted ownership or authenticity. Seals played an important part of everyday life in the ancient world; they were commonly used in the home and the marketplace, not only for security but for quality verification of natural products. Ancient people also used personal, seal symbols to mark their identity.

The stamp and the cylinder are the two main types of seals used in the ancient world. The stamp type of seal is flat and an impression is made by pressing it downward into the clay or wax. The cylinder seal makes an impression by being rolled over the clay or wax.

FOOTNOTES: Chapter One: Sports in the Aegean

1.      *The Palace of Minos at Knossos*, Sir Arthur Evans, published by
        Biblo and Tannen, New York, 1964. Volume 3.
2.      Thukydides, *Historiae*, Book 1,4.1.1 (Minos)
3.      Bull-wrestling was called *Taurokathapsia* by the ancient Greeks.
4.      Ibid. #1, page 225.
5.      *Krete*, Nanno Marinatos, published by D.&I. Mathioulakis, Athens.
        It is Dr. Marinatos' theory that the bull represents a fertility god.
6.      Ibid. #1, page 204.
7.      Ibid.
8.      Ibid. #1, pages 223-224; and *Antiquity*, "The Cretan Bull Sports,"
        Anne Ward, (1968): pages 117-122. There is evidence of a fence at the
                Palace of Knossos thought to be for protection of spectators at bull games
                performed within the palace.
9.      Ibid. #1, page 182.
10.     Ibid. #1, page 210. This phase was circa 18-15th cen. B.C.,
        according to the Penguin Dictionary of Archaeology.
11.     Ibid. #1, page 212.

# CHAPTER TWO

## PANHELLENIC GAMES

Panhellenic Games were characterized by the participation of athletes and spectators from all areas of ancient Greece. The four Panhellenic Games were: The Olympic Games, which were the first and most famous of the games, were renewed in 776 B.C. and ended in circa 394 A.D.; the Pythian Games, circa 582 B.C. to circa 300 A.D.; the Nemean Games, the first recorded game took place in 573 B.C. and ended circa 394 A.D.; and the Isthmian Games, which were reorganized from a local competion to a panhellenic competition between 582 to 570 B.C. and ended circa 394 A.D. A truce was declared for a time before, during, and after the games, so those attending could travel to and from the games in safety.

We believe women were competing in all the Panhellenic Games, and in the Olympic Games they were competing through the Heraean Games, which were held around July/August, and were a festival honoring the goddess Hera, consisting of foot races for girls. The Heraean Games were probably held around the same time of year as their male counterparts. Also, we believe women were competing as their own charioteers in some of the major games.

As today, even though the women's and men's games all come under the same heading, the Olympic Games, there were separate games for women for most of the events.

Small, bronze statues have been found that match Pausanias' description of the clothing worn by the girls at the Heraea; however, there have not been any inscriptions referring to the Heraean winners at Olympia found to date. (figure 12&13) Chloris, who is mentioned as the first winner in the

Figure 12 – Bronze figure of an ancient girl runner, now located in the Athens Archeological Museum.

Heraea, is the only name mentioned in ancient literary sources on the Heraean Games.

We know women were taking part in all the Panhellenic Games because we have inscriptions that have been found with the names of women winners. Some of the inscriptions give the name of the winner, the game in which she won, and the event. Other inscriptions are fragmented and may not give all the information.

Three of the Panhellenic Games were located on the Peloponnese: Olympic, the Nemean, and the Isthmian Games. The Pythian Games were located in Delphi in the area of Phokis, in central Greece. All the games were held in honor of the Olympian goddesses and gods, such as Hera, Demeter, Zeus, and Apollo.

The games were held in different years so they did not overlap. This was done so the importance of each game was not diminished, and to allow the games to have a good attendance and the participation of all the athletes. Crowns made from vegetation indigenous to the areas of the different games were presented to the winning athletes. In most of the games, other than the

Figure 13 - "Bronze figure of a running girl" Greek, about 520–500 B.C., found at Prizen, Serbia; possibly made in Sparta, Greece. Located in the British Museum, London, © British Museum.

Panhellenic Games, the crown was made of palm, and in all of the games a palm leaf was placed in the right hand of the winner.[1]

All the games were ended by 394 A.D., during the reign of Christian Emperor Theodosios I, because they were considered to be a pagan tradition.[2]

FOOTNOTES: Chapter Two: Panhellenic Games

1.      Pausanias, Description of Greece. Translated by J. G. Frazier. Bk VIII. 48.2.
2.      Nikolaos Yalouris, Archeologist and former General Inspector of Antiquities of
        Greece, said it is a possibility that the games ended during the reign of Theodosios
        II, around 424 A.D.

# CHAPTER THREE

## THE OLYMPIC GAMES

The Olympic Games held in 776 B.C. were the first recorded games. Plutarch, an ancient Greek historian who lived from 46 to 120 A.D., wrote that Hippias, who was a fourth century B.C. Greek sophist, compiled the first list of winners from the Olympic Games held in 776 B.C. Plutarch writes that the chronology of the list is uncertain, since Hippias wrote at a much later date.[1]

Hippias, compiling the names of the 776 B.C. Olympic winners several hundred years after the event took place, would not have known for sure how long the games had been taking place before this date. Nobody would have known, so it makes sense he would start with 776 B.C. as the first game.

Credit for the ancient renewal of the Olympic Games is given to Iphitos, a king of the territory of Elis, who probably lived around the ninth century B.C. Pausanias writes that Lykurgos, who created the Spartan laws, was a contemporary of Iphitos and helped him arrange a truce for the games to be held.[2] Kleisthenes, who was the king of Pisa at that time, also helped with the truce.

Pausanias describes seeing the "quoit of Iphitos" upon which the truce was written. A quoit was a flat disk usually made of stone or metal. *"On the quoit of Iphitos is inscribed the truce which the Eleans proclaim at the Olympic festival: The inscription is not in a straight line, but the letters run round the quoit in a circle."* [3]

The crown awarded the winning athletes was made of wild olive branch.

## 776 B.C. NOT THE FIRST OLYMPIC GAMES:
## A THEORY OF THE AUTHORS

Any dates for the beginning or renewal of the Olympic Games are theoretical. Information for dating the games is limited and scholars can only guess at a possible timetable. We have devised the following theory based on the end of Troy VII in approximately 1190 B.C., which is thought to be the date for the destruction of the Troy in Homer's epic poem, the *Iliad*. [1] By tracing forward in time from an ancestor that can be placed at Troy VII to their descendants, who lived at the time the first series of Olympic Games ended, we can create a plausible time frame. To develop this time frame more fully we have used information from the ancient sources to count backward in time from the date of 776 B.C., which is thought to be the date of the first recorded Olympic Games.

The date of 776 B.C. was not the first of the games to be held in a renewed Olympic Games that had, according to Pausanias, been discontinued for a period of time[2]; but, it was the first in which the names of the winners were recorded.

Pausanias states that the games were discontinued after the reign of Oxylos, who was king of the territory of Elis where the games were held. Oxylos had been told by an oracle to share his throne with a descendant of Pelops, who was said to have originated the games.[3] Oxylos found Agorios, who was the great, great grandson of Agamemnon, who was Pelops' grandson. (see Descendants of Pelops page 43)

Agamemnon, according to Homer's *Iliad*, was the commander of the Greek forces in the Trojan War. If this is true then he must have lived no later than circa 1190 B.C, since that is an accepted date for the end of the Trojan War.[4] Therefore, with his great, great grandson, Agorios being five generations removed from Agamemnon, and a generation in ancient times being 25 years,[5] Oxylos and Agorios must have lived no later than 1065 B.C. So, if the games were discontinued after Oxylos' reign, they were discontinued circa 1065 B.C.

Pausanias writes that the Olympic Games were discontinued down to the time of the Elean king Iphitos, who renewed the games.[6] Phlegon of Tralles, a second century A.D. historian, writes that there were 28 Olympiads from the time of Iphitos until the time of Korebos, who was a cook from Elis and the first recorded winner in the 776 B.C. Olympic Games.[7]

If we are to believe Phlegon that there were 28 Olympiads, which equals 108 years (the games occurred every four years starting with game one) from Iphitos to Korebos then, we can date the time of the first game in Iphitos' renewed Olympic Games to 884 B.C. by adding 108 years to 776 B.C. This also makes Korebos the winner of the 28th Olympiad and not the first Olympiad in the renewed series of games.

By subtracting Iphitos' renewal date for the games of 884 B.C., from the date the original series of the Olympic Games were ended in 1065 B.C., we get 181 years for the amount of time the games were discontinued from the time of Oxylos to Iphitos.

1. Oxford Classical Dictionary, Third Edition, published by Oxford University Press, New York, 1996, edited by Simon Hornblower and Antony Spawforth.
2. Pausanias BK V. IV. 5.
3. Pausanias BK.V.IV.3
4. Oxford Classical Dictionary, Third Edition, published by Oxford University Press, New York, 1996, edited by Simon Hornblower and Antony Spawforth.
5. A generation in ancient times was 20 to 30 years, we're using 25 years.
6. Pausanias BK V.VIII.5.
7. Scriptores Rerum Mirabilium Graeci, published by Brunsvigae, London,1839, Phlegon of Tralles, Olympic Chronicle, BK I.5,6.

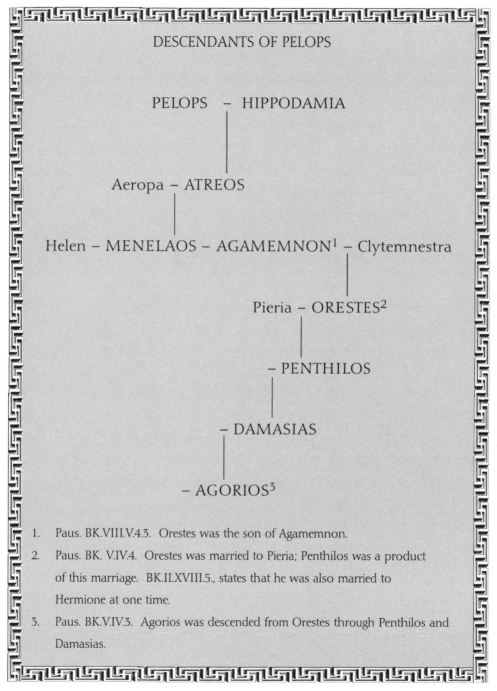

DESCENDANTS OF PELOPS

PELOPS – HIPPODAMIA

Aeropa – ATREOS

Helen – MENELAOS – AGAMEMNON[1] – Clytemnestra

Pieria – ORESTES[2]

– PENTHILOS

– DAMASIAS

– AGORIOS[3]

1. Paus. BK.VIII.V.4.3.  Orestes was the son of Agamemnon.
2. Paus. BK. V.IV.4.  Orestes was married to Pieria; Penthilos was a product of this marriage.  BK.II.XVIII.5., states that he was also married to Hermione at one time.
3. Paus. BK.V.IV.3.  Agorios was descended from Orestes through Penthilos and Damasias.

## ORIGIN OF THE OLYMPIC GAMES

The actual beginning of the Olympic Games is not known. However, there are several origin myths:

## THE MYTH OF HERKULES

According to Pausanias, Herkules and his four younger brothers, Paeoneos, Epimedes, Iasois, and Idas, came from Ida, on the island of Krete, to the area which was to become known as Olympia. Herkules, for the fun of it, had his brothers run a race and the winner was crowned with a wild olive branch, probably, because it was so plentiful they were even using it to sleep on. Herkules gave the name Olympic to the race.[4] This story has become one of the traditions of the origin of the Olympic Games.

## THE MYTH OF PELOPS AND HIPPODAMIA

If the citizens of the ancient Greek city-state of Pisa had placed bets on the odds favorite to win in the nineteenth chariot race for the hand of the Princess Hippodamia, they would have lost their "chimations,"[5] or as the saying goes "shirts." Eighteen times suitors tried to beat Oenomaos, the King of Pisa, in the chariot race for his daughter's hand, and eighteen times they not only lost the race but their lives.[6]

The story, according to Pausanias, is as follows: Oenomaos was the King of Pisa, which was a wealthy, ancient Greek city-state located in the vicinity of Olympia. He had a beautiful, unmarried daughter, Hippodamia, who was probably made even more appealing because of her father's wealth. An oracle, who is a person that can fortell the future, had told the King that he would be killed by his son-in-law, which is one of the reasons Oenomaos was unwilling to have his daughter marry.

Since Hippodamia had so many suitors, Oenomaos devised a plan that would prolong her status as a single woman. He promised her hand in marriage to whoever could beat him in a chariot race. The race was to be run from the Kladeos River, in Olympia, to the altar of Poseidon on the Isthmo s of Korinth, which is a distance of about 80 kilometers. At her father's request, Hippodamia, would ride in the chariot of her suitor, probably as a distraction to slow him down, since Oenomaos would give him a head start.

Once the suitor and Hippodamia started out, Oenomaos would sacrifice to Zeus, and then spear in hand, start after them with his charioteer, Myrtilos, guiding the horses. The King, because of the speed of his horses and the skill of his charioteer, was always able to overtake the suitor and kill him. Eighteen suitors died this way and their heads were fastened over the door of the palace to discourage others. (figure 14) Having your head hanging above the king's doorway might discourage some, but not the brave Pelops.

Pelops was from Lydia, in Asia Minor. Apparently, he was not only brave but clever. He found out that Myrtilos was secretly in love with Hippodamia but didn't have the courage to enter the competition against Oenomaos to win her hand. Pelops promised Myrtilos that if he let him win he would allow him to spend one night with Hippodamia.[7] In this way Pelops was able to bribe Myrtilos to cither, leave out some axle pins in one of Oenomaos' chariot-wheels, or substitute the bronze pins in the axles for wax. Whatever the method he used, the result was during the race one of the wheels of Oenomaos' chariot fell off sending the chariot crashing to the ground and killing him. (figure 15)

Pelops, as winner, married Hippodamia and became king of Pisa. He, also, annexed the City of Olympia, which had been part of the territory of Elis.

To celebrate their marriage Pelops instituted the Olympic Games for the men to honor Zeus, the head of the gods of Olympos; and Hippodamia, with the help of the "Sixteen Women,"[8] instituted the Heraean Games for the women to honor Hera, Zeus' wife.[9]

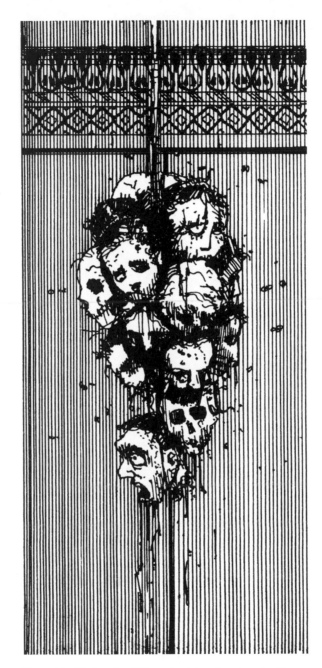

Figure 14 – The heads of Hippodamia's suitors hanging from
Oenomaos' door.

Myrtilos' fate was not as happy as Pelops'. Pelops still had the problem of keeping his side of the bargain with Myrtilos. When they were out sailing one day Myrtilos reminded Pelops about his promise to let him spend a night with Hippodamia. Upon being reminded Pelops pitched Myrtilos overboard and he was drowned. This short boatride was just enough time for Pelops to eliminate the problem of Myrtilos.

Pausanias lists the descendants of Pelops. (see Descendants of Pelops page 57) The most notable of these descendants is his grandson, Agamemnon, who can be traced to the Trojan War through Pausanias' books,[10] and the *Iliad* by Homer.[11]

The case to prove that Pelops and Hippodamia actually existed is strengthened by this list of descendants given by Pausanias, which includes Agamemnon. Agamemnon is also mentioned as the commander of the Greek forces at the Trojan War. Since Heinrich Schliemann uncovered the ancient site of Troy the likelihood of Agamemnon to have existed is strengthened. Through him we can set a time frame rising out of the Trojan War. We can go two generations back to Hippodamia and Pelops, Agamemnon's grandparents; or follow his descendants to the time of his

Figure 15 – The chariot race between Pelops and Oenomaos ending
in disaster for Oenomaos.

# PEDIMENT FROM THE TEMPLE OF ZEUS

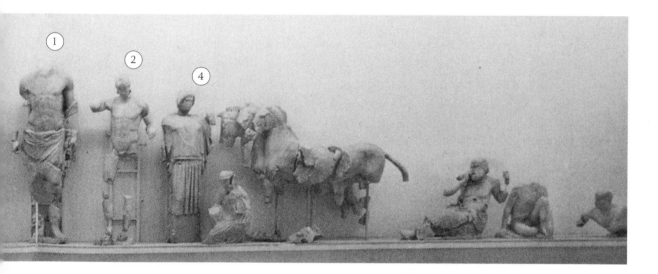

Sculptures from the east pediment of the temple of Zeus, showing the participants in the chariot race between Pelops and Oenomaos. Located in the Olympia Museum, Greece.
(1) Zeus
(2) Oenomaos
(3) Pelops
(4) Hippodamia or Sterope (Hippodamia's mother,) it is not known which statue represents which woman
(5) Myrtilos (kneeling)

great, great grandson, Agorios, who shared the throne with Oxylos, the last king to hold the Olympic Games until the time of Iphitos.[12]

(See page 48-49, Pediment from Temple Zeus)

## THE SIXTEEN WOMEN

Hippodamia is given credit by Pausanias for assembling a group of women called the "Sixteen Women" to help her in organizing the Heraean Games to honor her marriage.[13] These women were to become so trusted that they were later called upon to handle matters of great importance, such as, a peace agreement between Pisa and Elis.

The story of the "Sixteen Women" is as follows: Prior to the time of Oenomaos, Pisa had been ruled by the tyrant, Damophon. Damophon had caused considerable problems for his neighbors the Eleans, who were the people living in the area of Elis. When Damophon died the people of Pisa told the Eleans they had nothing to do with the trouble Damophon had caused and wanted peace.

The Eleans, also, wanted to forgive and forget. To settle their differences and create the peace, the Eleans called together one woman, the eldest and most respected, from each of the sixteen cities in Elis. This assembly was called the "Sixteen Women," and they succeeded in their task of creating peace between the Pisans and the Eleans.

The significance of the story of the "Sixteen Women" is that it shows women were held in high esteem; so much so, they were entrusted to arrange the peace between the cities. The tradition of the "Sixteen Women" continued for hundreds of years, down to the time of Pausanias. He writes that during his time there were only eight of the original sixteen cities remaining, so two women from each city were picked to keep the initial number.[14]

Pausanias writes, *"every fourth year the 'Sixteen Women' weave a robe for Hera and the same women also hold games called the Heraea."*[15] This passage informs us that the Heraean Games were held every four years, as were the Olympic Games. The games consisted of footraces for girls or virgins, which Pausanias called unmarried girls. The girls were divided into three age groups. The groups ran according to age with the youngest running first. Pausanias gives a firsthand account of the runners during his time:

*"The virgins are not all of the same age. The youngest run first, the next in age run next, and the eldest virgins run last of all. They run thus: Their hair hangs down, they wear a shirt that reaches to a little above the knee, the right shoulder is bare to the breast."* [16] (figure 16, 17a, b)

The girls used the same course as the men, the Olympic stadium, only the length of the course for their race was shortened by one-sixth. The winners would receive the same prize as the men, *"crowns of olive and a share of the cow, which is sacrificed to Hera."* [17] They, also, could have their names engraved on statues of themselves and dedicate them in their honor in the temple of Hera. (figure 18)

Figure 16 – Drawing based on Pausanias' description of girls running in the Heraean Games.

Figure 17 a, b – Statue, considered to be Atalante, dressed as Pausanias' description for girl runners. Located in the Vatican Museum, Rome.

Figure 18 – Reconstruction model of ancient Olympia, located in the Olympia Museum, Greece. 1) Temple of Zeus, 2) Temple of Hera, 3) Stoa of Echo

## THE HERAEAN FESTIVAL

It is our belief that the Heraea in Ellis was the women's counterpart to the men's Olympic Games. Hippodamia's and Pelops' marriage celebration is a probable starting point in the Olympic Games for men and the Heraean Games for women to be held together, with the Heraean Games being continued as the female Olympics.

No one knows the origin of the Heraean Festival; it is likely it was originated much earlier than the time of Hippodamia and Pelops. Heraean Festivals were held in a number of different areas of the Peloponnese. The origin of the festival was most likely connected with the cult of the goddesses Demeter Chamyne and Fiskoa, both deities reflecting the agrarian life-style of Peloponnesian society with their main occupation being farming.

The farmers were at the mercy of the natural elements such as weather. Bad weather could destroy their entire crop, leaving them to starve. Therefore, with their livelihood at stake, and in an effort to feel a sense of security and control over the uncontrollable, they held festivals in which they honored a "Mother Goddess," who represented life and fertility. Through these festivals they hoped to insure the fertility of their crops and a good harvest.

Down through time the "Mother Goddess" was known by various names. It is likely the deity Hera was an outcome of these "Mother Goddess" cults and she became the deity worshipped and celebrated in festivals for fertility. Hence, the name of the Heraean festival comes from the goddess Hera.

It is possible that the Heraean Games held in other areas of the Peloponnese, eventually, were held in conjunction with the other Panhellenic men's games. Since the Heraea was limited to footraces, it could be; women's chariot races were most likely combined with the men's races in some of the games.

## THE STORY OF CHLORIS:
## THE FIRST WOMAN TO WIN AT THE GAMES

Some say it was murder. Some say it was the plague. Whatever it was that killed ten of Meliboea's siblings [18] was traumatic enough to permanently turn her a deathly pale. She became so pale that her name was changed to Chloris, meaning "the pale woman" in ancient Greek. Chloris was the daughter of King Amphion, the King of Thebes. Her mother was said, by Pausanias, to be Pelops' sister Queen Niobe, which made Chloris Pelops' and Hippodamia's niece.

When Hippodamia instituted the Heraean Games, Chloris was the first woman to win in the games.[19] Pausanias writes that he saw a statue of Chloris in the sanctuary of Latona, which was by the sculptor, Praxiteles.[20]

## THE STORY OF KALLIPATIRA

Pausanias describes the penalty for a woman if caught attending the Olympic Games on forbidden days.

*"On the road to Olympia, before you cross the Alpheos (River), there is a precipitous mountain with lofty cliffs as you come from Scillos. The mountain is named Typaeon. It is the law of Elis to cast down from this mountain any women who shall be found to have crossed the Alpheos on the forbidden days."*[21]

Another phrase of Pausanias' makes one wonder if he always distinguishes between married and unmarried women by using the words women and maidens. When using the word women is he always referring to married women only, since women can mean any adult female human being, married or unmarried?

The definition for maidens (virgins) is an unmarried, young female so we know that Pausanias, when referring to maidens always means unmarried. The following paragraph gives an example of how

Pausanias uses these words:

*"Even maidens may ascend as far as the prothusis, and women too, when they are not excluded from Olympia.*[22]

If Pausanias always means married women when he speaks of women, it could mean that only married women were banned from crossing the Alpheos River on certain days; and unmarried women, or maidens, could always cross the river and attend the games.

Pausanias relates the story of Kallipatira, which demonstrates the law forbidding women to cross the Alpheos River on certain days and attending the games. As Kallipatira, or Pherenike [23] as she was also called, entered the house she could feel how tired she really was. She had taken over her son Pisirothos' training after her husband, Kallianax,[24] had died a few months previously. Her husband, like the rest of her family, had been an Olympic winner and they had hopes that Pisirothos would follow in his footsteps.

Kallianax and Pisirothos had been working on Pisirothos' wrestling skills and felt sure he would carry on the family's Olympic tradition. But when Kallianax died all seemed lost until Kallipatira made the decision to train Pisirothos herself. After all, she had acquired the knowledge of how to prepare an athlete for competition from growing up with a family of athletes and watching them train all her life. Now, she could put that knowledge to work so that her son could finish his training and compete for the sake of his dear father's memory and the honor of the family.

The day of the Olympic Games Kallipatira knew she was not allowed in the stadium to attend the games; only maidens, or virgins, and the Priestess of Demeter were allowed. It would mean so much for her to see Pisirothos win. She knew that he would want her there. She also knew that the penalty for any married woman, which she was considered to be, breaking the rule and attending the games was death by being thrown from the Typaeon Mountain to be crushed on the rocks below.[25] How would they know she was there if she disguised herself as one of the male trainers? They wouldn't.

All she had to do was to keep quiet and leave the minute Pisirothos' wrestling match was over.

Everything worked like a charm. Her son was winning and the crowd was going wild. Kallipatira could hardly contain her enthusiasm and every now and again would let out a little yelp. When Pisirothos finally won it was just more than she could bare. In the excitement of the moment she leaped over the barrier of the trainers area into the arena, and in doing so exposed herself as a woman to the shock of the crowd. (figure 19) Such a mixture of emotions she felt; jubilation at the victory and fear at the rage of the throng of men converging on her.

The judges, after taking into consideration Kallipatira's family tradition of Olympic competition, decided they would not punish her. There is not any record of any woman ever being thrown from the Typaeon Mountain, and it is unlikely this penalty was ever carried out.[26]

It is our belief that Pausanias was referring to particular days and events of the Olympics, during which the law forbade women to cross the Alpheos River and attend the games. Pausanias never mentions the reason behind this law. There were other days and events of the Olympics that he makes it quite clear that unmarried women, which Pausanias calls maidens or virgins, were allowed to attend. Pausanias states:

*"Opposite the umpires is an altar of white marble: on this altar a woman sits and beholds the Olympic games; she is the Priestess of Demeter Chamyne, an office conferred from time to time by the Eleans on different women. But they do not hinder maidens from beholding the games."* [27]

Unmarried women did not need to participate in the men's Olympic stadium events because they held there own games, in the same stadium, through the Heraea.[28] They most likely were allowed to attend the equestrian events since they, as well as the men, could own the competing horses and chariots. Some of these women owners were, also, the breeders. The owners were listed as the winners in the races; however, they did not drive their chariots but, instead used hired charioteers.

In the beginning, all winners in these chariot races were the owners not the charioteers, although this may have changed as time went on. There is evidence that women drove their own chariots in other festivals and Panhellenic Games. (see Sparta – Hyakintheia Festival, and Isthmian Games)

Figure 19 – Drawing depicting Kallipatira leaping over the trainers rail at the Olympic Games and exposing herself as a woman.

# WOMEN WINNERS IN THE OLYMPIC GAMES

## THE STORY OF KYNISKA

During the time of Agesilaos, who was the son of the Spartan King Archidamos, wealthy Spartan men took much pride in breeding their horses for the Olympic games. Horse-breeding and racing were popular activities among the wealthy Spartans at the time, and the fashion during the fourth century B.C. was for owners to hire charioteers to race for them and then claim the victory for themselves. Plutarch writes that *"Agesilaos regarded it as a display not of any real virtue, but of wealth and expense."*[29]

Agesilaos, decided to teach his friends and countrymen a lesson by showing them that it didn't take any special skills to win. Anyone could win the chariot races at Olympia if all they had to do was to provide the chariot and horses and hire a charioteer to race them. He persuaded his sister, Kyniska, to enter her chariot and horses in the race. Kyniska was a passionate horse breeder and a great lover of the Olympic Games, so she was probably happy to be asked by her brother to participate.[30]

Agesilaos obviously thought that by having a "mere " woman win in the games would lessen the importance of winning and make the men see how silly they had been for taking pride in that which they did so little work. His scheme backfired. Kyniska won and judging from all the honors she received for winning it appears she was viewed as a heroine. Kyniska became the first woman to breed horses and win a chariot race at the Olympic Games. She won in the chariot event in 392 B.C., which was the 97th Olympic Game, counting from 776 B.C.[31] A shrine was dedicated in her honor and she was worshipped in Sparta.[32] Most importantly, Kyniska became a role model for other women to compete with their chariots and teams.

Pausanias, in Olympia, describes seeing statues of Kyniska, her bronze chariot and horses, which he says were smaller than life-size,[33] and her charioteer, all of which were the work of the sculptor Apelleas.[34]  The pedestal of Kyniska's statue is the only remnant of the statues that exist today and is located in the Archeological Museum at Olympia. It is made of black limestone, and there are impressions on the top that could be indications of where the feet of her statue had been. (figure 20) The inscription, Olympic inscription number 160, on the front of the pedestal of Kyniska's statue reads:

"My fathers and brothers (are) the Kings of Sparta. I, Kyniska, won in the chariot race with swift-footed horses. I erect this statue and I say that I am the only woman from all of Greece who has ever won this crown. Made by Apelleas, son of Kallikles."

Figure 20 - "Pedestal of Kynisca." Located in the Olympia Museum.

## EURYLEONIS

Pausanias writes of seeing a statue of Euryleonis, a woman winner in the Olympic Games in the two-horse chariot race. This statue was located in Sparta on a hilltop in what was called the Acropolis, or upper city.[35]

## VELESTEHE

Velestehe won at the Olympic Games twice.[36] Once in the four-colt chariot race, and once in the two-colt chariot race. She was a woman from Macedonia and the mistress of King Ptolemy II Philadelphos, who was the ruler of Egypt.

Velestehe first won at the Olympic Games in the four-colt chariot race. This victory is documented in the Oxyrhynchus Papyrus number 2082, fragment 6. It is believed to have been the first of her two victories by the editors of the Oxyrhyncus Papyri, Professor Hunt and Professor Grenfell.[37]

According to Pausanias, Velestehe won in the two-colt chariot race in the 128th Olympiad;[38] and according to Professors Hunt and Grenfell, the 128th Olympiad occurred in 268 B.C.[39]

## KASIA

Another woman Olympic winner was Kasia Mnasithea. In the summer of 1989, at the ancient site of Olympia, a fragment was found of an inscription with the name of a woman winner in the chariot race in 21 A.D.[40] The name of this winner was Kasia Mnasithea, who was from the territory of Elis.[41]

*"Kasia Mnasithea, daughter of Marcus Vetlenus Laetus, won in the chariot race in Olympia in the … (now known to be the 200th Olympiad)... Olympiad in honor of Olympian Zeus."* (Olympic inscription no. 233)

Kasia and her family were very involved in their community and in the Olympic Games. Her grandfather, L. Vetlenus Laetus, was a benefactor to the community. Kasia's father, Marcus Vetlenus Laetus, proposed honorary citizenship for a famous pancratiast (boxer-wrestler) to Elis, and also asked permission from the Olympic Council for the pancratiast to be allowed to erect a statue to honor himself.

## THEODOTA ANTIPHANOS

Olympic inscription number 203 relates,
*"Theodota Antiphanos, from Elis, won in the chariot race with colts."*

## TIMARETA

Timareta, who was the daughter of Olympic winner Theodota Antiphanos, won an Olympic victory with a team of horses. Other members of Timareta's family were also involved in the Olympic Games. Her grandfather, Antiphanos, was the president of the Olympic Hellanodikae, who were the judges of the games. Her father, Philistos, was an Olympic victor with a team of horses, as was Timareta. Timareta'a brother honored his sister and mother by dedicating a statue to them. The inscription on the statue, Olympic inscription number 204, reads:

*"...Strogien the sons of Philistos dedicate to the Olympian Zeus (the statue) of the sister Timareta, and altogether (the statue of) Theodota, the mother."*

Olympic inscription number 201 states that Timareta won with a team of horses:

*"Timareta from Elis, daughter of Philistos, won with a team of horses."*

## THE FATE OF THE ANCIENT OLYMPIC GAMES

The Olympic Games deteriorated and the last game was held in 392 A.D. With the spread of Christianity the games, which were considered pagan practices, came to an end.[42]

According to John Malalas, a sixth century A.D. Syrian historian, the right to hold the Olympic Games was sold by the Pisians to Syria for ninety Olympiads, or 360 years. Syria first celebrated the games in the Syrian province of Antioch, in the third century A.D.[43]

Malalas wrote that *"young people of noble birth"* came from all over the ancient Greek world to compete in these games, and many of them were girls.[44] The girls *"were present under a vow of chastity, competing, wrestling in leggings, running, declaiming and reciting various Hellenic hymns. These women fought against women and the competition was fierce whether in the wrestling, the races or the recitation."*[45]

The Byzantine Emperor Justinian, in 521 A.D., restored the right to hold the Olympic Games to the territory of Pisa. However, the games were never held in ancient Greece again, because Olympia was destroyed by an earthquake soon after.

Could the participation of girls in the Olympic Games held in Syria have been the continuation of their participation, through the Heraean Games, in the Olympic Games held in Olympia, Greece?

## OLYMPIC STADIUM AND HIPPODROME

### THE STADIUM

The word stade in ancient Greece meant a unit of length measuring 600 ancient feet, which equals 192.27 meters [46] and approximately 631 feet. A stadium in ancient Greece was a course for footraces with its length based on one stade.

According to Professor Nikolaos Yalouris,[47] archeologist and former

General Inspector of Antiquities of Greece, the stadium at Olympia went through three phases, Stadiums I, II, and III. (figure 21)

Stadium I, built during the Archaic period 600 – 480 B.C., was a simple, rectangular form without any embankments on the sides.The finishing line, open to the Altar of Zeus, was at the narrow western end of the course.

Stadium II, can also be dated to the Archaic period. Its position was similar to the first stadium, but was moved further east putting the track on a lower level. The two long sides of the stadium had embankments making easier viewing for the spectators.

Stadium III, dated to the early fifth century B.C., was moved east 82 meters, and north seven meters. The narrow, western end was closed in, and excavations have shown that after the mid-fourth century B.C. the western end embankment was shortened to allow for the Stoa of Echo to be built. The Stoa of Echo was an elongated building, walled at the back, with two rows of colonnades at the front and rooms at the far end. The building had the qual-

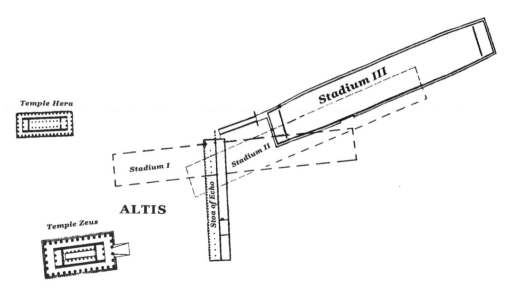

Figure 21 - Reconstruction drawing showing Stadiums I, II, III at ancient Olympia

ity to reverberate sounds seven times. This quality gave it the name *Heptaechos*, which means seven echoes in Greek.[48]

The only seats in the stadium were of stone and reserved for important people such as the Hellanodikai, who were the judges, and the Priestess of Demeter, which was an honorary position bestowed on different women from time to time by the people of Elis.[49] The rest of the spectators, estimated to have been up to 45,000 people, sat on the embankments.[50] (Figure 22)

Building the Stoa of Echo isolated the stadium from the sacred areas of the sanctuary, to which it had always been connected. Professor Yalouris states, with the separation of the stadium from the rest of the sanctuary the nature of the games began to change and lessen in their religious significance.

A tunnel–like corridor called *Krypte* was added in the late third century B.C., which once again connected the stadium to the sanctuary. The *Krypte* was used by the athletes and the Hellanodikai as the official entrance to the stadium. (Figure 23)

Figure 22 – Ancient stadium at Olympia as it appears today.

Figure 23 – The *Krypte*, a tunnel-like corridor, connected the stadium to the sanctuary at Olympia.

## THE HIPPODROME

The word hippodrome consists of two ancient Greek words: hippo, which means horse; and drome, which means race. The Olympic Hippodrome was located between the stadium and the Alpheos River, and over the course of time all traces of it have been washed away by the river. Nothing exists of the hippodrome from ancient Olympia  and we must rely on ancient writings for any information.

Pausanias writes that if you leave the stadium from the area where the umpires sit, which was in the middle of the riverside embankment where the spectators sat, you will come to the hippodrome and to that area which is the starting-place for the horses. The shape of the hippodrome is that of a u-shape with a colonnade called the Colonnade of Agnaptos, after the architect who built it.[51]

The Colonnade of Agnaptos squares off the open end where the horses start. The lengthwise division of the course into two parts by two turning posts connected with rope between them, allowed the length of the course to be doubled. This division started about halfway down the course so the horses could start the beginning of the race in a ship's prow formation. The prow's broad end was across the front of the Colonnade of Agnaptos, with the point of the prow heading all the racers to one side of the divided course. (figure 24)

The competitors would draw  lots for starting position stalls that were in the sides of the prow formation, which were over four-hundred-feet long. A barrier rope was stretched in front of the stalls. In the middle of the prow was a bronze eagle on an altar and  in front of the point of the prow was a dolphin on a rod. When a starter made the eagle jump the dolphin fell to the ground and at that time the barrier rope dropped first for the horse closest to the colonnade. When this horse came abreast of the horse next in order the rope was dropped for him, and so on until all the rope had been dropped and all horses were racing. This system was invented by Kleotas.[52]

The horses would turn the post at the u-shaped end of the course and race back on the other side of the divider. Pausanias informs us that on one of the turning posts there was a bronze statue of Hippodamia. Apparently, it looked as if she were about to decorate Pelops for winning with a ribbon she was holding.[53]

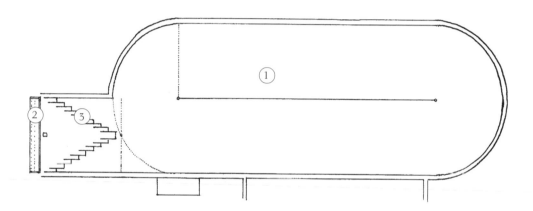

Figure 24 - Diagram of the ancient Olympic hippodrome.
    1) Rope connected between two posts
       devides the course into two parts.
    2) Colonnade of Agnaptos.
    3) Starting point in the shape of a ship ís prow.

## NERO AND THE OLYMPIC GAMES

Greece became a Roman province in 146 B.C. During the time of Roman Emperor Nero, the games were in danger of losing their significance. Nero, in 65 A.D., attended the games in Olympia not only as a spectator but as a contestant. With 5,000 Roman troops, which he brought to support him, Nero entered the games. Guess who won? Nero. When Nero fell from his chariot in the chariot races, the other contestants graciously waited for him to remount and cross the finishing line as the winner.[1]

Another story relates that Nero's chariot turned over during the race and that the other racers continued on. Nero got up and finished the race. Although, he was not the first one over the finishing line he was still awarded the first prize, since the judges said he would have won if his chariot had not turned over.[2]

Needless to say, Nero won most of the olive crowns.

Roman Emperor Nero

1.  C. Robert Paul and Jack Orr, *The Olympic Games.*

2.  Arthur Weigall, *Nero, The Singing Emperor of Rome.*

FOOTNOTES: Chapter three: The Olympic Games

1.  Plutarch, *The Lives of the Noble Grecians and Romans*, NUMA POMPILIUS, para. 1, Dryden Translation, published by William Benton, 1952.)

2  Paus. BK. V.IV.5.

3.  Paus. BK. V.XX.1.

4.  Paus. BK. V.VII.6-7,9.

5.  *Chimations* is the ancient Greek word for shirt.

6  Paus. BK VI.XXI.7. The number of Hippodamia's suitors is taken from a list given by Pausanias.  He got the list of suitors from a poem he read called, *Great Eoeae*, by the ancient Greek poet, Hesiod. This poem no longer exists.

7.  Some, i.e. *Cromwell's Handbook of Classical Mythology*, believe that it was Hippodamia's idea to bribe Myrtilos.  We agree with this because who would be in a better position to know Myrtilos' feelings for her and to suggest to the suitor of her choice the idea of bribery. She probably thought she would never get married at the rate her father was dispensing with suitors, and she wasn't getting any younger.

8.  Paus. BK.V.XVI.4.

9.  A theory, supported by Curtius, *History of Greece*, is the Heraea originated before Hippodamia's establishment of the games to celebrate
her marriage.

10.  Paus. BK II.IV.2.

11.  Homer, The *Iliad*, lines 130-140.

12.  Paus. BK V.VIII.5.

13.  Paus.BK V.XVI.4.

14.  Paus. BK.V.XVI.7.

15.  Paus. BK.V.XVI.2.

16.  Paus. BK V.XVI.3.

17.  Ibid.

18.  Paus. BK V.XVI.4.

19.  Paus. BK V.XVI.4. Chloris was victorious at the first Heraea.  She probably won in the footraces, since that was the only race we know of in the Heraea.

20.  Paus. BK II.XXI.9, Pausanias describes seeing a statue of Chloris in the Sanctuary of Latona still in existence during his time, second century A.D.

21.  Paus. BK V.VI.7.

22.  Paus. Bk V.XIII.10.

23.  Paus. BK.V.VI.7.

24.     Paus. BK VI.VII.2. Pausanias does not make it clear that Kallianax was the father of Pisirothos. Pausanias does say Kallianax was Kallipatira's husband and the father of her son, Eucles. It is possible he was not Pisirothos' father.

25.     Paus. BK V.VI.7. No woman was ever thrown from the Mountain. Pausanias writes that Kallipatira was the only woman ever caught breaking the law and she was not thrown off the Mountain because her family had distinguished themselves at the Olympic Games for generations. Most likely, no woman would have been thrown off the Mountain anyway.

26.     Kallipatira was also known as Pherenike, according to Pausanias, *Descriptions of Greece* BK. V. 6. 7-8. Also, Pherenike means to bring victory in Greek, which leads one to believe Pherenike was the name given to Kallipatira after her exploit. There has been confusion over the two names, Kallipatira and Pherenike. Some scholars believe they are two sisters.

27.     Paus. BK VI.XX.9.

28.     Paus. BK. V.XVI.3.

29.     Plutarch, *The Lives of the Noble Grecians and Romans, Agesilaus.*

30.     Paus. BK.III.VIII.1.

31.     Paus. Bk III.VIII.1, BK III.XV.1. Kynisca won in the chariot event.

32.     Paus. BK III.XV.1.

33.     Paus. BK V.XII.5.

34.     Paus. BK VI.I.6.

35.     Paus. Bk.III.XVII.6.

36.     The name Velestehe, when translated, has various spellings, such as, Belistiche, Belestiche, Bilistiche.

37.     Oxyrhynchus Papyri, Part XVII, edited by Arthur S. Hunt.

38.     Paus. BK.V.VIII.11.

39.     In Frazer's translation of Pausanias, BK.V.VIII.11, he writes that Velestehe's (Belistiche's) win occurred two Olympiads earlier than the 131st Olympiad, however, in the actual ancient Greek text her win occurred three Olympiads before the 131st Olympiad.

40.     Luigi Moretti dates Kasia's victory to approximately the second half of the second century A.D. An article from Archaeological Reports For 1989-1990, *Olympia*, by E.B. French, states that in 1989 excavators in Olympia unearthed a fragment of an inscription, which had been part of a victory statue for an Elian woman named Kasia. This fragment helped to complete an already discovered inscription telling of Kasia's victory. The new fragment placed Kasia's win at the 200th Olympiad, which means she won in 21 A.D. and not the date suggested by Moretti.

41.     Archaeological Reports for 1989-1990, No. 36. Published by The Council of the

Society for the Promotion of Hellenic Studies, and The Managing Committee of the British School of Athens, 1990. Archaeology in Greece, Olympia, pg. 30.

42. Stephen Miller, Professor at Berkley and archeologist in charge of excavations at Nemea, Greece, states that it is not known when exactly the Olympic Games were ended. He goes on to say that there were two Roman emperors named Theodosios and both of them were concerned with wiping out pagan practices, which is believed to have brought about the end of the games.

43. The Chronicle of John Malalas, A translation by Elizabeth Jeffreys, Michael Jeffreys and Roger Scott, pages152-153. Malalas writes that the Olympic Games were sold in 260 A.D. This date conflicts with the date that the last winner was crowned in the Games in Greece, 369 A.D.

44. The Chronicle of John Malalas, A translation by Elizabeth Jeffreys, Michael Jeffreys and Roger Scott, pages 152-153.

45. Ibid.

46. Kl. Palaeologos, *The Olympic Games in Ancient Greece, Running* , page 174.

47. Nicolaos Yalouris, *Olympia*, pages 14-15.

48. Ibid., page 22.

49. Paus. BK VI.XX.9.

50. Ibid., page 15.

51. Paus. BK VI.XX.10-15.

52. Ibid., pages 10-14.

53. Paus. BK VI.XX.10. Hippodamia's statue.

# CHAPTER FOUR

## THE PYTHIAN GAMES

## THE ORIGIN OF THE PYTHIAN GAMES

Delphi, the site of the Pythian Games, is located in Phokis in central Greece and is the longest established community in the area.(figure 25) Ancient Delphi was famous for its oracle, which originally referred to a place in Delphi where vapors with mystical qualities were emitted through a chasm in the earth. The ancient Greeks flocked to the oracle to receive its mystic revelations and advice given by a woman who became known as the Oracle of Delphi. She was called the Pythia and was appointed to the position of oracle to channel messages from the god Apollo, which supposedly emanated from the vapors. (figure 26)

Some scholars believe that Pythia told the future by seeing it in a basin of water, which was on a tripod, or by chewing laural leaves to induce a trance–like state allowing her to have visions of the future.

As recently as August 2001, a professor of Earth Sciences at Weseleyan University in Connecticut, J.Z. de Boer, and John Hale, an archeologist at the University of Louisville in Kentucky, published their findings supporting the theory of a vaporous chasm in the earth from which the Pythia inhaled and was then able to give her predictions. They found new faults that they traced to below the covered Sanctuary which intersected with old segments of the Delphic fault. Gases were found coming from the faults, one of these gases was ethylene, which produces narcotic effects, thus substantiating the myth of the oracle inhaling vapors from the earth.

Homer in his works, the *Iliad* and the *Odyssey*, refers to the area of Delphi as Pytho.[1] The word Pytho comes from the ancient Greek verb *Pythomai*, which means to decay or to inform. According to mythic tradition, Delphi is known by this name because the god Apollo killed the dragon (serpent,)[2] who guarded the oracle, and left its body to rot.[3] The Pythian Games began as a musical contest to celebrate Apollo killing the dragon.[4]

Apollo became the god of Delphi and spoke through the oracle. Individuals and government delegations sought advice from the oracle. The oracle's influence was felt throughout Greece, and Delphi became a sacred sanctuary.

Figure 25 - Aerial view of Delphi showing the ancient stadium site near the top of the hill, and the Valley of Krissa, located below, where the ancient hippodrome once existed.

## THE PYTHIAN GAMES

The Pythian Games originally were held every eight years and the organization of the games was in the hands of the citizens of Delphi. In 582 B.C., the organizers of the games[5] were changed to ten or twelve tribes of Greece, which were called the Delphic Amphictiony (similar to the present day United Nations.) The games, under the Delphic Amphictiony, started being held every four years, which fell in every third year of each Olympiad. The

month was August/September, known in ancient times as *Boukatios.* From the fourth century B.C. on, the games were held in October, known in ancient times as *Heraios.* They lasted about six to eight days. A three-month truce was declared at the time of the games so people could travel safely to and from the games. Also, they were reorganized to include athletic and equestrian competitions.

The names of the Pythian victors were inscribed on stone tablets. The winners were crowned with laurel leaves.[6]

Figure 26 – Drawing of Pythia, the oracle of Delphi, inhaling the vapors from a chasm in the earth.

## WOMEN WINNERS IN THE PYTHIAN GAMES

Hermesianax could not have been more proud. All three of his daughters had been victorious at some of the most prestigious games. He knew his daughters were special when each was born, regardless of what his friends said about it's being better to have sons. He wanted to show his daughters and the world how much he loved them and now he stood looking at the result of this desire, statues carved from the finest marble of the three triumphant women. They were magnificent! Hermesianax gazed at the statue of each daughter and relived their moment of victory and the joy he felt at each game when his daughter's name was called and she was crowned victorious.

Only the base of the statues survived and was found in Delphi. On the base the statues of the three, young women must have stood, and the inscription reads:

### TRYPHOSA

*"Hermesianax, son of Dionysios, citizen of Caesarea Tralles and also of Korinth, erected these statues of his daughters, who themselves also hold the same citizenship.*

*Tryphosa won the footrace at the Pythian Games when Antigonos and Kleomachidas were the organizers of the games, and the footrace at the ensuing Isthmian Games when Iouventios Proklos was the organizer of the games, (Tryphosa was) the first of the virgins.*

*Hedea won the race for war chariots in armor at the Isthmian Games when Cornelius Pulcher was the organizer of the games, and the footrace at the Nemean Games when Antigonos was the organizer of the games, and at Sikyon when Menoitas was the organizer of the games, she also won the competition for singing with the guitar in the boys category at the Sebasteia in Athens when Nouios, son of Philinos, was the organizer of the games.*

*Dionysia won in Isthmia [7] (The location of Isthmia is thought to be where Dionysia won. However, it is not totally clear the name of the event is lost,) and won in the footrace at the Asklepeia in sacred Epidavros when Nikoteles was the organizer of the games."*

The inscription for all three sisters has been entered under the Pythian Games, even though only one sister won at Delphi. The inscription should be read together so one can understand their father's pride in such remarkable daughters.

## THE END OF THE PYTHIAN GAMES

In 373 B.C., an earthquake destroyed the list of the Pythian victors. Aristotle, a fourth century B.C. Greek philosopher, and his nephew Kleisthene drew up a new list. The Pythian Games continued through Roman times until circa 394 A.D., when the oracle was closed down and the destruction of the temples was ordered. With the spread of Christianity the games, which were believed to be pagan, were banned.

## THE STADIUM

The sanctuary and stadium at Delphi are located on a terraced hillside with the stadium above the sanctuary. Originally all athletic and equestrian contests were held on the plain of Krisa, which is in the valley below the later hillside stadium. The stadium was constructed in the second half of the fith century B.C.

The Delphic stadium (figure 27) was 178.35 meters from the runners starting-point to the finishing line, whereas the stadium at Olympia was 192.27 meters. The width of the track allowed seventeen to eighteen runners to run abreast. An embankment bordered the track on the uphill side where spectators could sit and watch the games. Stone seating for around 7,000 spectators was built into this embankment in the mid-second century B.C.

Figure 27 – The ancient stadium at Delphi as it appears today.

## THE HIPPODROME

The ancient hippodrome was located on the Plain of Krisa, which was located in the valley below Delphi. Nothing of the ancient hippodrome is in existence today and no one knows the actual location of the hippodrome on the Plain of Krisa.

FOOTNOTES: Chapter Four: The Pythian Games

1.  Paus. BK X.VI.5.  Pausanias writes that Homer calls Delphi Pytho.
2.  Ibid.  Apollo killed dragon.
3.  Paus. BK X.VI.6.  Dragon guarded oracle.
4.  Paus. BK X.VII.2.  First contest was musical.
5.  The organizers of the games were called *agonothetae,* in ancient Greek.
6.  Paus. BK VIII.XLVIII.2.
7.  Dittenberger, *Sylloge Inscriptionun Graecarum,* Volumen Alterum, pg. 495.

# CHAPTER FIVE

## THE NEMEAN GAMES

### THE ORIGIN OF THE NEMEAN GAMES

According to Pausanias, the Nemean Games originated with Adrastos, king of Sikyon. (Sikyon is close to Nemea and Argos.[1] Also, Homer's epic poem, *The Iliad*, describes Adrastos as the former king of Sikyon.[2] The fact that Homer mentions Adrastos in *The Iliad*, dates Adrastos to the Trojan War, which ended circa 1190 B.C. Therefore, the Nemean Games probably originated circa 1190 B.C.; however, the first recorded Nemean Game was in 573 B.C.

The Nemean Games were held in honor of Opheltes, the infant son of King Lykurgos of Nemea, who had died. The following is the story of Opheltes.

Opheltes was in the care of his nurse, Hypsipyle, when the "Seven Against Thebes," who were seven generals on their way to conquer Thebes, came upon her and asked for water. Hypsipyle put the baby Opheltes on the ground and went off to fetch the water for the generals. While she was gone, Opheltes was bitten by a snake and died. When Adrastos, the leader of the generals, and the other generals found the dead baby they killed the snake and buried Opheltes. They thought the death of the baby was due to them and was a bad omen. Therefore, they declared the Nemean Games to be held in honor of Opheltes.[3]

## THE NEMEAN GAMES

While traveling around the Peloponnese in the area of Nemea where the Nemean Games were held, Pausanias writes:

"Adjoining the temple of Apollo is also the stadium in which they celebrate the games in honour of Nemean Zeus and the games of Hera."[4]

From this statement of Pausanias we learn that women and men at Nemea shared the same stadium for their games. Could it be that the Heraean Games were the women's counterpart in the Nemean Games as we, the authors, believe they were in the Olympic Games? The Heraean Games only consisted of running and, therefore, the women would have had to compete directly in the Nemean Games if they wanted to participate in equestrian events.

The Nemean Games were reorganized from local games to a Panhellenic Game in 573 B.C.[5] Stephen Miller, the American archeologist in charge of the excavations at the Nemean Games site, states that between the late fifth century B.C. and the decade of the 330's B.C. there was not any activity at the Nemean site.[6] He believes that the games were moved to Argos, an area south of Nemea, during this time and later moved back to Nemea.

Professor Miller believes the games were moved back to Nemea in the 330's B.C. by the Macedonians, during the time of Philip of Macedonia and his son, Alexander the Great. He believes this was done in an effort to unify the Greeks by reviving their old panhellenic centers.[7] The stadium, the Temple of Zeus, and many other buildings were built in Nemea after the 330's B.C.

Around 316 B.C. the Argives appointed "theorodokoi," who were from the local area and acted as greeters for the visitors to both the Nemean and the Heraean Games.[8]

According to Pausanias the Nemean Games were celebrated in the winter.[9] The games were celebrated every two years. The prize was a crown of celery in honor of Archemoros, which was another name for Opheltes.[10]

## WOMEN WINNERS IN THE NEMEAN GAMES

### HEDEA

*"Hedea won...in the footrace at the Nemean Games when Antigonos was agonothetes..."*
Hedea also won in two other games, the Isthmian Games and at a contest in Sikyon. (see Pythian Games for complete inscription)

### VERENIKE II

*"I have a song of victory to sing: for news has just come from Argos to Egypt, that at Nemea, in the chariot race, your horses won..."*
Verenike II was Queen of Egypt and the ancient Greek poet, Kallimachos, wrote the above inscription as part of a poem in which he memorializes her victory as the owner of the winning chariot.[11] The original inscription fragments have been reconstucted by scholars to form the above quote.

### THE STADIUM

Stephen Miller describes the game site at Nemea as consisting of the Sanctuary of Zeus and the stadium. (figure 28) The hippodrome has not been found. Miller, in his 1977 excavations at Nemea, discovered a vaulted passageway similar to the passageway at the stadium in Olympia. He describes this tunnel-like passageway as being cut into the hill on the west side of the track. The passageway was 2.07 meters wide, 2.48 meters high, and ran 36.35 meters long from the race track to the other end, which is in the direction of the Sanctuary of Zeus a quarter mile away.[12]

Miller suggests that the tunnel may have been used as a place for the athletes to change out of their clothes, as the custom of the day was to compete in the nude, before they ran into the stadium when their name was announced. Athletes running out of the passageway into the stadium must have created a dramatic entrance, which would have thrilled the spectators.[13]

The latest possible date for the tunnel's construction is 320 B.C. This belief of Miller's is partly due to being able to date names mentioned in graffiti, which was found scratched in the passageway walls.[14]

The stadium's southern end is in a horse-shoe shape built into a hillside with the race track extending out from this on a manmade jut of land to its northern end. The stadium could accommodate more than 40,000 spectators.[15]

Miller and P. Valavanis, from the University of Athens, in a joint effort during the summer of 1993 at Nemea, reconstructed the starting mechanism, called the *hysplex*, which was used to start the runners at the ancient stadium.

The *hysplex* mechanism consists of wooden frames set into the stone starting bases. These wooden frames had rope torsion springs attached to them, which means the rope is in a twisted condition and will return to its natural straight condition when released, thus allowing enough pressure on the barriers in front of the runners to be dropped and give them a simultaneous start.

This reconstructed model of the *hysplex* mechanism for starting was tested using high school students from Nemea and California. The model worked perfectly, showing that the knowledge of the *hysplex* mechanism, which had been lost for centuries, has been rediscovered.[16] (figure 29)

Figure 28 – Photograph of present day Nemea showing the stone starting line.

Figure 29 – High school girls from Nemea and California tested a reconstructed model of the hysplex.

FOOTNOTES: Chapter Five: The Nemean Games

1.  Paus. BK X.XXV.7, BK II.VI.6.
2.  Homer, *Iliad* , BK 2.572.
3.  Perseus Program, Tufts University, Pseudo-Apollodorus, Library vol 1.359.
4.  Paus. BK II.XXIV.2.
5.  Oxford Classical Dictionary, third edition.
6.  Stephen G. Miller, *Hesperia*, "Kleonai, the Nemean Games, and the Lamian War," Suppl. X Princeton, 1982, page107.
7.  Stephen Miller, *Hisperia*, "The Theorodokoi of the Nemean Games", April/June, 1988, page 163.
8.  Ibid., page 161.
9.  Paus. BK II.V.3.  Winter games.
10. Pseudo-Apollodoros, vol. 1.359, Perseus program, Tufts University; Paus. BK VIII.XLVIII.2.
11. Zeitschrift fur Papyrologie und Epigraphik, P.J.Parsons, Callimachus, Victoria Berenices, 25, page 6-7, (1977.)  Another Greek translation for Callimachus is Kallimahos, and for Berenice it is Verenike.
12. Stephen Miller, *Archaeology*, "Tunnel Vision: The Nemean Games," January/February, 1980, Vol. 33, Nbr. 1. page 54.
13. Ibid., page 54, 56.
14. Ibid., page 54.
15. Ibid., page 54, 56.
16. Stephen Miller, Archaeological Reports for 1993-1994, *Nemea*, pg.15.

# CHAPTER SIX

## THE ISTHMIAN GAMES

### THE ORIGIN OF THE ISTHMIAN GAMES

The origin story of the Isthmian Games is told by Pausanias. He writes that the games were originated as funeral games to honor the child Melikertes. After Melikertes' father, in a fit of rage, killed his elder brother, Melikertes' mother hurled both herself and him into the sea. A dolphin took the boy's body and put him on the Isthmos of Korinth, where he was found and his name was changed to Palaemon. King Sisyphos of Korinth instituted the Isthmian Games in Palaemon's honor.[1]

### THE ISTHMIAN GAMES

The Isthmian Games owe their importance to their close proximity to the city-state of Korinth, whose citizens organized and ran the games.

Korinth, known in the ancient world as Ephyraea, is located on the Peloponnese near a narrow strip of land called the Isthmos of Korinth, which joins the Peloponnese to central Greece. (figure 30) The Korinthians took advantage of their strategic location by developing a flourishing trade with the western and eastern areas. Korinthian trade was extensive and their economy was diversified due to their fertile agricultural land and crafts-men skilled in working with bronze and clay. They became the wealthiest city-state in ancient Greece by 750 B.C., which they maintained with only two short interruptions for over 1,000 years.

The Isthmian Games started as local games and were reorganized as a Panhellenic Game around 582 B.C. The games were organized by the Korinthians until 146 B.C., when Korinth was destroyed. After Korinth's destruction the neighboring people of Sikyon took over the responsibility of organizing the games. When Korinth was rebuilt, in 44 B.C., the Korinthians again reorganized the games and held them every two years.

## WOMEN WINNERS IN THE ISTHMIAN GAMES

### TRYPHOSA

*"Tryphosa won...the footrace at the...Isthmian Games when Iouventios Proklos was agonothetes..."*

Tryphosa also won at the Pythian Games. (see Pythian Games for complete inscription)

### HEDEA

*"Hedea won the race for war chariots in armor at the Isthmian Games when Cornelius Pulcher was agonothetes..."*

Another winner at the Isthmian Games was Tryphosa's sister, Hedea. (see Pythian Games for complete inscription)

### DIONYSIA

*"Dionysia won in Isthmia..."*

Dionysia, like her sisters Tryphosa and Hedea, won in Isthmia. (see Pythian Games for complete inscription)

## THE STADIUM

Stone slabs pave the starting point for the runners, which is the only section of the Isthmian stadium remaining from the classical period. This starting point is in the shape of an isosceles triangle. One person controlled the runners start. This person stood in a hole at the tip of the triangle and held the ends of ropes, which were attached to bars positioned in front of the runners, who stood side-by-side in a line at the base of the triangle. When the starter dropped the ends of the ropes the bars fell allowing the runners to start.

Archeologists have uncovered the starting and finishing points of a stadium dating to the Roman and Hellenistic periods. This stadium was built in a hollow at the foot of a small hill named, Rachi. The length the stadium was 181.15 meters, which is shorter than that of the Olympic stadium, which was 192.27.

## THE HIPPODROME

A fifth century B.C. Athenian poet and playwright, Euripides, wrote in his play, *Hippolytos*, that the hippodrome at Isthmia was on a long stretch of hard sand on a silvery beach. The Isthmian hippodrome has long since vanished and we only have ancient references for descriptions.

Figure 30 – Korinth (Korinthos) is in a stategic location on the Isthmos of Korinth, which joins the Peloponnese to central Greece.

FOOTNOTES: Chapter Six: The Isthmian Games

1.      Paus., BK II.I.3; VIII.XLVIII.2.

# CHAPTER SEVEN

## THE STATUS OF WOMEN IN ANCIENT GREECE

The social status of women in ancient Greece cannot be generalized, since it varied not only from one area to another, but from one time period to another.

The Minoan civilization worshipped the "Mother Goddess" as the supreme deity, who represented fertility and life. Their worship of this female deity combined with the Minoan's artistic depiction of women in socially prominent positions leads one to assume that women held a high status in Minoan society.

"Mother Goddess" worship continued into the Mycenaean period and eventually the worship of a male deity, called Zeus, was added.

Greece developed into independent city-states each with their own form of government and laws. These ancient city-states were characterized by continual warring between them with an occasional alliance for their mutual benefit. The connections that bound them together as Greeks were a common language and religion.

Two of the city-states, Sparta and Athens, were at opposite ends of the social and political spectrum with city-states, such as; Korinth, Thebes, and Sikyon falling somewhere in-between. There was a great diversity in the status of women in the different city-states. Women's status was no longer determined by their society's form of worship. Instead, each city-state had separate laws and was ruled independently, and depending on what these laws were determined the status of the women who lived there. There were always those individual women who, no matter what type of society they lived in, managed to attain achievements beyond the social limitations of her time and place.

A common mistake in the study of ancient Greece is that writers tend to base their information on the ancient Athenian's way of life. Since Athens was the cultural Mecca of ancient Greece, most of the information on ancient Greece is from writers who lived in Athens and wrote from an Athenian point of view. The problem with this is Athenian society was an exception among city-states.

Sparta was another city-state that was an exception. All aspects of Spartan life were directed towards creating a strong military state. Athenians, on the other hand, centered their lives on philosophical, political, and artistic pursuits.

## ATHENS

Unlike Sparta, the Athenians encouraged creativity in the arts, philosophy, architecture, and science. Participation in athletics was foreign to the women of Athens. They did not take part in most public demonstrations of social or political life. However, they did go out in public to attend the theater, which was an educational experience, since this was where social ideas were often presented in the form of plays. They also participated in philosophical debates, but not in public.[1]

Even in Athenian society there were women who were allowed to attend various schools and excel as students. One such example was Themista. In Athens, Themista attended a school of philosophy run by Epikuros, who was a third to fourth century B.C. Greek philosopher. Epikuros held the school in his house and Themista developed a reputation as an excellent student. Themista became so well-known and respected for her wisdom that in the first century B.C. Cicero, who was a Roman statesman and philosopher, used her as a standard of comparison when he wrote: "...even though you may be wiser than Themista."[2]

Most Athenian women centered their lives around their family and home. They lacked an independent status apart from men and their primary roles were that of a wife and mother. Women were always under the legal guardianship of a father, husband, brother, son, or some other male relative.

## SPARTA

Sparta, also known in the ancient world as Lacedaemon, was the capital of the area of Laconia, located on the Peloponnese. Since the Spartan's did not write any accounts of history, the history of ancient Sparta comes from non-Spartan sources such as Pausanias, Herodotos, Thukydides, Aristotle, Plutarch, and others. Therefore, the history of Sparta may reflect the positive or negative attitude of the writer towards Sparta.

Sparta's political and social life was based on a militaristic society. The main purpose of all Spartan's from childhood to adulthood was to serve the needs of the state. The main need was a strong military. Therefore, the best way they could serve the state was to be mentally and physically prepared to protect it. Women were equal to men in all areas of Spartan life but one, they could not join the military and go to war.

Lykurgos, a ninth century B.C. king of Sparta and founder of the Spartan constitution, emphasized in his laws physical training for girls, as well as boys.[3] Evidence of this can be seen in the writings of Plutarch, a Greek philosopher and  biographer who lived circa 50 – 120 A.D. Plutarch writes Lykurgos' reply "when someone else desired to know why he instituted strenuous exercise for the bodies of the maidens in races and wrestling and throwing the discuss and javelin, he said, 'so that the implanted stock of their offspring, by getting a strong start in strong bodies, may obtain a noble growth, and that they themselves may with vigor abide the birth of their children and readily and nobly resist the pains of travail; and moreover, if the need arise, that they may be able to fight for themselves, their children, and their country.'"[4]

This statement by Lykurgos, tells us Spartan women were expected to be as physically fit as the men in order to produce strong, healthy babies, who would become strong adults to better serve the state. Also, Philostratos, a Greek writer from the third century A.D., writes, "Lykurgos instituted female exercise to produce more and better warrior-athletes."[5]

Spartan physical training consisted of wrestling, footraces, and discus and javelin throwing. (figure 31) A statement by Plutarch mentioned previously in this chapter, lists these exercises as part of Lykurgos' training regimen. Wrestling was practiced in the nude by both girls and boys, and they competed together in footraces.

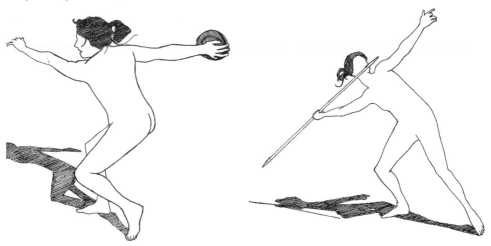

Figure 31 - Girls participated in discus and Javelin throwing in ancient Sparta.

Propertius, a Roman poet born circa 54 B.C., confirms that girls in the nude were taking part in wrestling by writing:

*"At the many laws of thy wrestling-grounds do I marvel, O Sparta, but most at the plenteous blessings of the schools where thy women train, inasmuch as a girl may without blame disport her body naked among wrestling men."[6]* (Figure 32, 33)

He further states that girls took part in a number of other sports such as: The *pancratium*, which was a type of unrestrained fighting combining boxing and wrestling; boxing, he describes a girl putting on boxing gloves; throwing the discuss; hunting; horseback riding; and sword fighting in armor.

*"...the woman stands at the race's furthest goal and endures wounds in the cruel boxing-match. Now she binds the glove to her hands that rejoice in its thongs, now swirls in a circle the discus' flying weight; now with hoar-frost sprinkling her hair she follows her father's hounds o'er the long ridges of Taygetos, now tramples the ring with her steeds, girds the sword to her snowy flank and shields her virgin head with hollow bronze..."* [7]

Spartan girls oiled their bodies, as did the boys, before they ran in races. (figure 34, 35) Girls racing can be seen in a poem written by a third century B.C., Greek poet named Theokritos. The poem is about Helen the bride of the Spartan king, Menelaos. She was the famous Helen, whose kidnapping was partly responsible for starting the Trojan War. The poem describes her earlier more carefree days as a young girl running footraces with the rest of the maidens, before she was married.

*"...For sure all we which her fellows be, that ran with her the race,*
*Anointed lasses like the lads, Eurotas' pools beside –*
*O' the four-times threescore maidens that were Sparta's flower and pride*
*There was none so fair as might compare with Menelaos' bride....*
*O maid of beauty, maid of grace, thou art a huswife now;*
*But we shall betimes to the running-place i' the meads where flowers do blow..."* [8]

It must have been believed during Theokritos' time that Spartan girls had been foot racing long before Lykurgos and his athletic regimen, since Helen and the Trojan War were hundreds of years earlier than Lykurgos' time.

Euripides, a fifth century B.C. Greek playwright, expresses outrage in his play, *Andromache*, about how the Spartan girls dressed when they went out with young men and their exercise habits.

*"Not even if she wanted to could a Spartan girl be chaste. They leave their houses in the company of young men, with bare thighs and loosened tunics, and in a fashion I cannot*

*stand they share the same running tracks and wrestling places with them."* [9]

The Spartan girls were called *phainomerides*, which means "bare-thighed," by Ibykos, a sixth century B.C. Greek lyric poet, and he classified them as nymphomaniacs. Plutarch maintained that Spartan girls did not appear naked for any other reason than their ingrained, true desire for the health and beauty of their bodies.[10]

Plutarch, who was open minded and pro-Spartan, remarked on the girl's tunic style dress, or *peplos* as it was called in ancient Greece. He said girls and women from other areas of Greece who wore the *peplos* would sew the side slit from the waist down, but the Spartan girls left theirs open and as they walked the material would fly back and reveal their whole thigh. (figure 36a,b) This must have been truly outrageous to the socially conservative Athenians.

Exercises of jumping in place called *bibasis* were also practiced. Aristophanes, an Athenian, comedic playwright who lived at the end of the fifth century B.C., wrote a play called, *Lysistrata*. Athens and Sparta were traditional rivals and enemies and through a character in the play called Lampito, Aristophanes makes fun of the Spartan women and their gymnastic training. The following excerpt has the Athenian, title character, Lysistrata, greeting the Spartan woman, Lampito.

LYSISTRATA:

      Good day, Lampito, dear friend from Lacedaemon. How well and handsome you look! What a rosy complexion! and how strong you seem; why, you could strangle a bull surely!

Figure 32 – Greek, bronze handle of a patera which is a shallow bowl used for offerings.
The handle shows a girl wearing a *diazoma*, which is an athletic loincloth.
From the second half of the sixth century B.C.
Located in the Metropolitan Museum of Art, Rogers Fund, 1946. (41.11.5a)

Figure 33 – Greek, bronze handle of a patera which is a shallow bowl used for offerings.
The handle shows a girl wearing a diazoma, which is an athletic loincloth.
From the second half of the sixth century B.C.
Located in the Metropolitan Museum of Art, Rogers Fund, 1946. (46.11.6)

Figure 34 – Greek bronze, mirror handle of a girl athlete holding an oil flask in her left hand, which was used by ancient athletes to hold the oil they used on their bodies. From the third quarter of the sixth century B.C. Located in the Metropolitan Museum of Art, Fletcher Fund, 1938 (38.11.3)

LAMPITO:

Yes, indeed, I really think I could. Tis because I do gymnastics and practice the kick dance.

Lampito, in her response, is referring to an exercise in the compulsory gymnastic training for Spartan women and men, in which they would kick their buttocks with alternate heels while hopping on one foot. (figure 37) The Athenians commonly joked about these exercises, and the humor in Aristophanes' play can still be appreciated today.[11]

Figure 35 – Bronze statue of a girl runner holding a strigil, which was used to scrape oil of the athletes body. Located in the Museum für Kunst und Gewerbe, Hamburg, Germany.

Figure 36a, b – Peplos worn by ancient Greek women.
      a) Depicts how Spartan girls wore the peplos.
      b) Depicts how Athenian girls and most of the
       girls in ancient Greece wore the peplos.

To be seen practicing or competing in the nude was a way of life in Sparta, and girls and boys were raised to be comfortable appearing nude in public. The laws of Lykurgos required the young women and men to participate nude in processions and choral dances; and on certain solemn occasions the young men were to watch the girls sing and dance nude. The songs the girls sung either derided or praised individual young men depending on their actions in war. The idea behind this law was to promote marriage by ostracizing the young men who continued to remain single from these processions and dances. The songs were meant to inspire the young men to greater glories in war.

The Spartan girl's nude, gymnastic training with the boys, along with their dress habits, and their nude participation in public celebrations, generated numerous scathing remarks by the Athenians, who found it all very shocking.

It is interesting to note that "*Gymnos*" is the ancient Greek word for naked. Gymnastics literally means, "exercises performed naked," and gymnasium is the building in which gymnastics are performed. The Spartans considered nudity the normal condition for practicing physical activities.

Lykurgos forbid his laws to be written down. He felt the laws that most affected the welfare of the people would find permanent security if the young people were brought up actually living the laws, which would imprint them in their hearts, instead of being taught their principles by just memorizing the written material.[12]

Around 195 B.C., Spartan independence and lifestyle, originally developed by Lykurgos hundreds of years earlier, came to an end with the domination of the Peloponnese by Macedonia and the Achaean League. The Achaean League was created in the 300's B.C., and it consisted of twelve Achaean cities located on the Peloponnese and in east-central Greece.

The Roman military invasion of Greece, in the 140's B.C., divided Greece

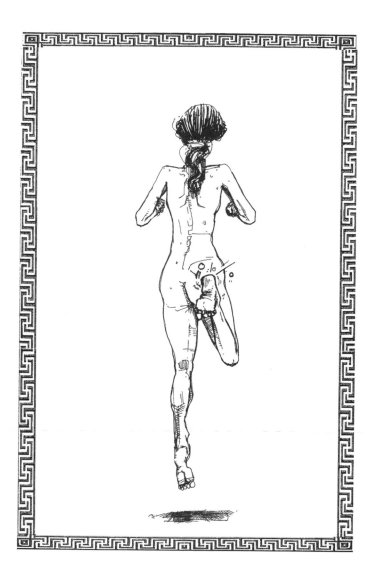

Figure 37 – Drawing depicting a girl doing the Spartan exercise
called bibasis, or butt-kick.

into provinces ruled directly from Rome. Rome admired the old customs of Lykurgos' Sparta. They declared Sparta a city free from the Achaean League, who had been allowed by Rome to continue ruling on their behalf.

Under Roman rule Sparta was allowed to re-institute Lykurgos' laws, and their culture became a tourist attraction.[13]

FOOTNOTES: Chapter Seven: The Status of Women in Ancient Greece

1.      Thukydides, *History*, II. 45.

2.      Cicero Against Piso 63 (Yonge) perseus.tufts.edu/

3.      The date for Lykurgos is not known, but we, the authors, have arrived
        at the time of circa the ninth century B.C. in our theory, "776 B.C.
        Not the First Olympic Games."

4.      Plutarch, Moralia III. 227.12, 13.

5.      Philostratos, De gymnasticus 27.1.

6.      Propertius, *Elegies*, BK 3.14.1, with an English Trans. by H.E. Butler.

7.      Ibid.

8.      Theokritos, *The Epithalamy of Helen*, XVIII.

9.      Euripides, *Andromache*, edited and translated by David Kovacs.

10.     Philostratus, De gymnastica 27.1.

11.     Aristophanes: *Lyszstrata*, The Panurge Press #146, New York.

12.     Plutarch, *The Lives of the Noble Grecians and Romans, Lykurgos,*page 38.

13.     *The Oxford Classical Dictionary*, edited by Simon Hornblower and Antony
        Spawforth, states that Sparta was the object of cultural tourism.

# CHAPTER EIGHT

## FESTIVALS

The ancient Greeks held numerous festivals to celebrate various religious and important community events. The contests in some of these festivals were in athletics, poetry, and singing. They provided an excellent opportunity for girls to take part in athletic contests. We have chosen to write about only a few of the athletic festivals, and only those in which we have evidence that women participated.

## THE ASKLEPEIA

The Asklepeia was a festival celebrated originally in Epidavros to honor Asklepios, who was born in Epidavros and was worshipped as a god. He was said to have been a great healer, who was even able to raise the dead.[1] Asklepios was worshipped in other areas of ancient Greece, but the most celebrated festival was in Epidavros. Every fifth year the festival was held nine days after the Isthmian Games.

## WOMEN WINNERS IN THE ASKLEPEIA

### Dionysia

*"Dionysia...won in the footrace at the Asklepeia in sacred Epidavros when Nikoteles was the organizer of the games."*

Dionysia and her two sisters, Tryphosa and Hedea, each won more than one contest. (see Pythian Games for complete inscription)

## THE AMPHIARAIA

The Amphiaraia was a festival celebrated at Oropos in honor of Amphiaraos, who possessed the gift of prophecy. Amphiaraos did not want to participate in a military expedition against Thebes, because he knew that he would be killed. However, he was persuaded by his wife to join the expedition. He fought bravely in the war against Thebes, but in his flight to get away from the enemy he and his chariot were swallowed up by a chasm in the earth near the area of Oropos. Amphiaraos could not escape his fate. Amphiaraos, who was from Argos, was deified by the people of Oropos. They were the first to worship him as a god, and later he was worshipped by all the Greeks.[2]

## WOMEN WINNERS IN THE AMPHIARAIA

### Avris

Inscription number 417, line 61 and 62, from Inscriptiones Graecae, edited by G.Dittenberger, gives the name of Avris as a woman winner in an equestrian event in the Amphiaraia. Avris' inscription states:

*"Avris, daughter of Kaikos from Kymi, won in the horse race with a full grown, male horse."*

### Lysis

An inscription carved in white marble, inscription number 140, lines 13 and 14, gives the name of Lysis as a winner in the chariot race.

*"Lysis, a woman from Magnesia and daughter of Ermonax, won in the chariot race with colts."*

## Mnasimaha

Mnasimaha, who was a woman from Thessaly, won a victory in the Amphiaraia. Inscription number 142, line 17, documents her win in the chariot race with colts. The white marble inscription reads:

*"Mnasimaha, daughter of Phoxinos from Kranon in Thessaly, won in the chariot race with colts."*

## THE ELEUTHERIA

The games called the Eleutheria, were held in Plataea in the territory of Boeotia. *Eleutheria* in Greek means "freedom," the games were called this in celebration of the defeat of the Persians, in 479 B.C., at Plataea. The Eleutheria was held every four years and the main contests were running.[3] The most famous race of the Eleutheria was the long distance race in full armor, which was run outside the stadium.

## WOMEN WINNERS IN THE ELEUTHERIA

### Aristokleia

Aristokleia was a woman from Larissa, who won in an equestrian event at the Eleuthereia. Inscription number 526 [4] states:

*"Aristokleia, daughter of Megaloklis from Larissa, won with a chariot drawn by two colts."*

Ipioni

A.S. Arvanitopoullos, a Greek archeologist, wrote an article for *Revue de Philologie* #35, published in 1911, in which he gives the name of a woman winner in the Eleutheria. On page 125, line 17, of his article there is a description of the white marble inscription, which states:

*"Ipione, daughter of Polyxenos from Larissa in Thessaly"*

Kostas Gallis, in his 1988 article, *The Games in Ancient Larissa*, published in the book, The Archaeology of the Olympics, gives the name of the Eleutheria as the games in which Ipione won and states that she won with a chariot drawn by four horses.

The inscription was found in the city of Larissa embedded in the wall of a house, in which it was used as building material. It is not unusual to find ancient stone fragments recycled over and over again in the construction of a newer building.

# THE HERAEA
## (Also, see chapter on the Olympic Games, Pelops and Hippodamia)

The Heraean Festival in honor of Hera (figure 38), the goddess of fertility, appears to have been taking place in different cities on the Peloponnese during ancient times. This does not seem unusual since the cult of Hera was widespread throughout the ancient Greek world. Two other goddesses were also worshipped at Olympia, Gaia and Rhea. They were regarded as "Mother Earth" goddesses and their sanctuary was one of the most ancient at Olympia.[5] The worship of Gaia and Rhea most likely developed into the worship of the goddess Hera.

We do not know the origins of the Heraean Festival. However, we believe it is older than the time of Hippodamia, who mythology credits with instituting the festival in honor of Hera for the celebration of her marriage to Pelops. The ancient Greeks worshipped a Mother Goddess deity as far back as the Minoans, according to Sir Arthur Evans, archeologist and excavator of the Minoan site at Knossos.

The main source for information on the ancient Heraea is Pausanias, and this information is scanty at best. We know, from Pausanias, that the Heraea was held every four years, "Every fourth year the Sixteen Women weave a robe for Hera; and the same women, also, hold games called the Heraea."[6] The festival was comprised of footraces run by young girls.

Figure 38 - Goddess Hera, located in the Olympia Museum.

## WOMEN WINNERS IN THE HERAEA

The only name that anyone has ever found of a woman winner in the Heraean Games is from the accounts of Pausanias, and that name is Chloris. (See chapter on the Olympic Games, Pelops and Hippodamia.) Pausanias writes:

*"...Hippodamia...assembled the Sixteen Women, and along with them arranged the Heraean Games for the first time. ...Chloris, daughter of Amphion, was victorious..."*[7]

Chloris' win was in the footrace, since these were the only games in the Heraea, as far as we know.

## THE HYAKINTHEIA

There were not any major panhellenic games that took place in Sparta, but the most important festival in which there were athletic competitions was the festival of Hyakintheia held in Amyklae, an area in ancient Sparta.

The ancient festival of Hyakintheia was a festival commemorating the death of Hyakinthos, who was said to have accidentally been killed by the god Apollo.[8]

Women took part in the chariot races in the Hyakintheia, as described in a statement by Athenaeos, a third century A.D. Greek philosopher. Athenaeos writes:

*"...some of the girls were conveyed in wooden chariots, extravagantly adorned with vaulted wicker; the other girls, engaging in yoked-team chariot contests, led the procession..."*[9]

## THE PANATHENAEA

The Panathenaea was a festival held in Athens. It started as a local festival in honor of the goddess Athena. Over time, the festival grew to encompass all the Attic communities, which were the areas surrounding the city of Athens.[10]

One of the main features of the festival was a procession to the Acropolis in which women carried an embroidered peplos, which was a shawl-like garment, to dedicate to the goddess Athena. All the people of Athens would participate in this precession to honor the goddess Athena. Maidens participated in the procession by leading chariots and sacrificial animals.

Peisistratos, who was a tyrant of Athens in the sixth century B.C., reorganized the festival into a Panathenaic Festival in 566 B.C. He added chariot races, horse races, music, and poetry to the festival.

The prizes in the equestrian events were *amphorae*, which were tall, narrow necked jars, filled with olive oil.

The biggest prize was given to the winner of the quadriga race, which was a race between chariots pulled by a team of four horses. This prize consisted of 140 amphorae filled with olive oil, which was enough for some of the winners to go into the olive oil export business. (figure 39) This is part of the reason why so many amphorae have been discovered around the Black and the Mediterranean Seas.

There were two categories of events, one in which only Athenians could take part, and the other which was open to everyone. The Athenian events were comprised of martial gymnastic contests, where the actions of soldiers in battle were imitated, and special equestrian events. The events, which were open to everyone, were based on the Olympic games program.

Considering Athenian society's attitude toward women, it is unlikely Athenian women were allowed to participate in the equestrian events; however, there are names of women winners in the equestrian events of the Panathenaic

Festival who were not from Athens.    Since these were not Athenian women, perhaps they were allowed to compete as contestants and not just the owners of the horses, as in the Olympic Games. We will probably never know. There is a fragment of a statue of a girl mounting a horse in the museum of the Acropolis of Athens. Could she have been a contestant in the equestrian events?

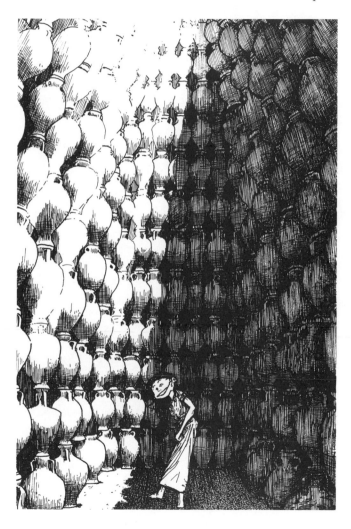

Figure 39 – The winners in the Panathenaea won enough jars of olive oil to put them in the export business.

## WOMEN WINNERS IN THE PANANTHENAEA

### Zeuxo, Eukrateia, Hermione, and Zeuxo (the mother)[11]

A mother and her three daughters won in the Panathenaea. The mother is Zeuxo from Kyrene. Kyrene is a city located on Cyprus, where Polykrates, the father, was governor. Their inscriptions are as follows:

*"Zeuxo, from Argos and daughter of Polykrates, won in the horse race with a full grown, male horse.*

*Eucrateia, from Argos and daughter of Polykrates, won in the chariot race with a full grown horse.*

*Hermione, from Argos and daughter of Polykrates, won in the... (contest unknown but probably a horse race).*

*Zeuxo, from Kyrene and daughter of Aristonos, won in the chariot race with a full grown horse."*

### Mnasiatha

Mnasiatha's inscription reads:
"Mnasiatha, from Argos, won in the chariot race with colts."

### Name Unknown[12]

The woman's name is missing on the inscription and it simply reads:
*"...a woman from Argos, won in the chariot race with a full grown horse."*

## NAME OF FESTIVAL UNKNOWN

Three names of women winners have been found in different areas of Greece, however, the name of the festival or Panhellenic Game in which they won is not mentioned.

### Eukleia

An inscription found on the island of Chios states:
*"Eukleia won in the chariot race with colts."*

### Damodika

An article in the *Bulletin de Correspondance Hellenique*, 1927, page 387, gives information about a stone epitaph found in the area of Kyma, in Aeolis. The epitaph is for a woman named Damodika, and states that she was a winner in an equestrian event.

*"Damodika, daughter of Kratis and wife of Hermogenis Asclepiades. My name is Damodika, my honorable husband is Hermogenis and my father is Kratis. On my death, I leave behind my son and the glory from my victory with a glorious chariot. On my death my husband was in Rome, so I missed the case to see him for the last time."*

### Nikegora

Manuel Souliardos, a humanist from Patras, which is on the Gulf of Korinth, Greece, wrote an annotation in the margin of Pausanias' manuscript. His annotation quoted an epigraph that he saw in the ruins of Patras, which was for a woman named Nikegora, who won in a footrace, and her brother, Nikofilos, erected a statue in her honor.[13]

*"I, Nikophilos, erected this statue of Parian marble to my beloved sister, Nikegora, victor in the girls' race."*

Unfortunately, the epigraph does not mention the festival or game in which Nikegora won. However, if her win had been in one of the more famous festivals her brother would probably have noted it.

## THE ISLANDS OF CHIOS AND LESVOS

## Chios

The same system of co-education that so clearly defined Sparta, existed on the ancient Greek island of Chios, in the Aegean Sea. Women shared an equal status with men and enjoyed the same freedoms. Athenaeos writes the following:

"The Spartan custom of displaying the young girls naked before strangers is highly praised; and on the island of Chios it is delightful just to walk to the gymnasia and running tracks to see the young men wrestling naked among the young girls, who are also naked."[14]

## Lesvos

On Lesvos evidence that girls were running in competitions is given in the writings of the greatest poetess of the ancient world, Sappho. (figure 33) Sappho was a Greek poetess, who lived on the island of Lesvos between 630 and 570 B.C. A small fragment of one of her poems states:

*"I was the teacher of Hero from Gyara, that fast girl runner."[15]*

FOOTNOTES: Chapter Eight: Festivals

1.     Paus. BK II.XXVII.4.
2.     Paus. BK I.XXXIV.2.
3.     Paus. BK IX.II.6..
4.     *Inscriptiones Graecae*, edited by Otto Kern, Volume IX, part 2, number 526, lines 19-20. Possible date, 196 B.C.
5.     George Eisen, *Sports and Women in Antiquity*, page 4.
6.     Paus. BK.V.XVI.2.
7.     Paus. BK V.XVI.4.
8.     Paus. BK. III.XIX.5.
9.     Athenaeos, Deipnosophistae 2,1.34-37,39.   Lines trans. by Jenny Beach, University of California at Irvine, Thesaurus Linguae Graecae.
10.    Paus. BK VIII. II. 1.
11.    Inscriptiones Graecae, edited by Udalricus Koehler, volume II, part II.  Zeuxo, pg. 385, lines 50-51. Eucrateia, pg. 385, line 5. Hermione, pg.385, line 39.  Zeuxo (the mother), pg. 388, lines 44 –45.)
12.    Ibid., pg. 388, line 54-55.
13.    Pausanias, ed. Fridericus Spiro, Berlin, 1900, p.137.
14.    Athenaeos, The Deipnosophists, translated by Charles Burton Gulick. Volume VI.XIII.566.
15.    Trans. by Kaldis-Henderson, *A Study of Women in Ancient Elis.*

# CHAPTER NINE

## THE MODERN DAY OLYMPIC GAMES

## MELPOMENE AND THE 1896 OLYMPIC GAMES

Her heart was beating as if it were in her throat; her breath was coming in short bursts. She was trying to calm herself and still keep the edge to her nerves, which would allow her a fast start when the signal was given. She would be running against the clock on the same course the men had run the day before.

From the first, when she heard that the Olympic Games were to be renewed and athletes from around the world were invited to compete, she became obsessed and dreamed of participating.

When she tried to register she was told by the all male Olympic committee that she had missed the deadline. She would run anyway! When the committee realized her intention they had talked her out of it by saying she could run in the women's race one week later. She had agreed to wait. The men ran their race without her. That was on Friday. It was now Saturday, the day after, and she prepared to race. Instinct told her not to wait longer.

The signal was given. As she lunged forward she was swept up in her own momentum and found herself falling into the rhythm of her race. Nothing could stop her! She was living her dream!

Various articles appeared in the March and April 1896 newspapers that carried the name of the woman runner, Stamata Revithi, some foreign papers calling her Melpomene, and told of her exploit. Most of these papers had covered her crusade to compete prior to the race. Stamata Rivithi was perhaps nick-named Melpomene [1] after the Greek muse of tragedy because of her poor and tragic background. She was 30 years old with a 17 month-old baby, extremely poor, and had a seven year-old child that died the Christmas prior to the race.

Stamata Revithi was slim, blonde, and had strong muscles from years of physical hard work. She had been living in the port of Pireas and was walking to Athens, with her baby, where she hoped to live and find work. On her way she met a young man who was walking to Athens for the exercise. He was the one who told her of the Olympic marathon race from the village of Marathon to Athens, [2] and encouraged her to enter. The idea of entering soon became an obsession when she heard that an American woman living in Athens, also, wanted to run. When Stamata applied to the Olympic committee for entry into the marathon she was told that she had missed the deadline for filing, as did the American woman.

Stamata decided to run unofficially in the men's race on Friday morning, March 29. That morning, Stamata asked the village priest to give a blessing for her to run fast; he replied that he would only read blessings for the official runners. When the Olympic committee found out about her plan to run without permission they talked her out of it by promising she could run a week later, on Friday, with a group of women runners. After agreeing not to run with the men, and missing the men's race, something occurred to make Stamata decide to run the next day, Saturday, March 30. Perhaps, she heard there was not to be a women's race and the committee had misled her to keep her from running, or maybe, it was just instinct.

Whatever compelled her to make the decision to run turned out to be right, since the women's race never took place. The mayor, a teacher, and the judge of the village signed a statement attesting to the time Stamata started the race. (figure 40) Five and one-half hours later, she finished the 40 kilometer race course. Her finishing time was recorded by several military officers she met near the stadium in Athens at the end of her race.[3] The finishing time of the winner in the race of the men was 2:58:50.

Stamata's race was not accepted officially and the Olympic Committee did all in their power to discourage and prevent her from running. The fact that she had the courage and determination to race, in spite of the committee and prevailing social attitude of the period against women in athletics, sent a message that women were not the helpless and inept creatures that were the fiction of the Victorian mindset of the 1900's.

Figure 40 – Depiction of Stamata Revithi, also known as Melpomene, on her run to Athens.

## AN UNSUCCESSFUl ATTEMPT
## TO RENEW THE OLYMPIC GAMES

In 1859 and 1870, a wealthy Greek named Evangelos Zappas, attempted to renew the Olympic Games. He held a national Olympics, which was called the "First Olympias," in Athens, Greece. The games were, also, known as "Zapios Olympias," probably since he sponsored them with his own money. These games failed to continue.

## THE 1896 OLYMPIC GAMES RENEWAL

The successful renewal of the Olympic Games in 1896, after a fifteen-hundred year absence, was the "brain-child" of Dimitrios Vikelas (1833-1908) (figure 41) and Baron Pierre de Coubertin (1863-1937.) (figure 42)

Dimitrios Vikelas, a renowned Greek immigrant, was born on the island of Syros, Greece, but lived in Paris, where he was recognized as a

Figure 41 - Demetrios Vikelas.

Figure 42 - Drawing of Baron Pierre de Coubertin.

writer, social worker, national benefactor, sportsman and visionary of the renewal of the Olympic Games, as well as, the first president of the International Olympic Committee.[4]

Baron de Coubertin, a 5'3" Frenchman, can be considered the first promoter of amateur sports on an international basis. Coubertin was born in Paris, where he attended L'Ecole Libre des Sciences Politiques (Free School of Political Science,) and studied liberal arts. He wanted to reform the French educational system and incorporate into it his philosophy that physical training and sports are essential in the formation of a student's character. Coubertin wrote about his ideas on physical training and founded several sporting societies. The French government, in the late 1880's, appointed him to form an international sports association. It was at this time Coubertin began his campaign to renew the ancient Greek Olympic Games.

In 1894, Coubertin, inspired by the idea of renewing the ancient Olympic Games, wrote numerous letters to sports organizations and news editors around the world. He traveled extensively to stimulate interest in his new passion and held large assemblies strategically located at historical sites to touch on the emotional aspect of reinstating the games with their historical significance. The "Congress for the Re-establishment of the Olympic Games," was organized to take place on June 16, 1894, in the grand amphitheater of the Sorbonne, in Paris. Invitations were sent out to athletic organizations worldwide, including the Panhellenic Gymnastics Organization in Athens, and 2,000 people attended. (figure 43)

The Panhellenic Gymnastics Organization was founded in Athens in 1891, and in "Article 2" of its constitution it states that, "the goal of the organization is the spreading of gymnastics to all social classes and the improvement of gymnastics." This goal would be pursued by the founding of the ancient Olympic Games, the creation of gymnasiums, and the publishing of writings on gymnastics. When the invitation arrived at the Panhellenic Gymnastics Organization, the organization accepted the invitation and Dimitrios

Vikelas was appointed to be its official representative.

The congress in Sorbonne lasted eight days, and in one of its sessions, in order to create the proper atmosphere, Madame Jeanne Remacle sang the "Hymn of Apollo." The hymn dated to 128 B.C. and had been excavated only one year earlier, in 1893, at the base of the "Athenian Treasury" in Delphi. Singing had been one of the first contests instituted at some of the ancient Greek games and festivals.

The work of the congress included eight topics of which seven focused on defining the word sportsman. The eighth topic was the only one that dealt with the renewal of the Olympic Games, which eventually became the main subject matter of the congress.

Dimitrios Vikelas was elected president of the Olympic Committee, and due to his title he was able to submit a memorandum and proposal suggesting that the first Olympic Games of 1896 should be held in Athens. The proposal was accepted with the help and great support of Pierre de Coubertin and the American representative William Sloan, a professor at Princeton University. Dimitrios Vikelas was, also, elected the first president of the International Olympic Committee (IOC) the governing agency of the Olympic Games, a position that he resigned in 1899.

According to the initial bylaws of the International Committee, a change of the position of president would occur every four years and a new president would be elected from the country chosen to host the next Olympic Games. These bylaws allowed Pierre de Coubertin to become the next president since the 1900 Olympic Games were to take place in Paris. Once Coubertin was president he changed the initial bylaws, which allowed him to remain president until 1925.

The 1896 Olympic Games rules did not ban women from competing; however, the Olympic Committee was successful in discouraging them from participating, as evidenced in the case of the woman Stamata Rivithi, mentioned earlier. No women participated in the 1896 Olympic Games. Women

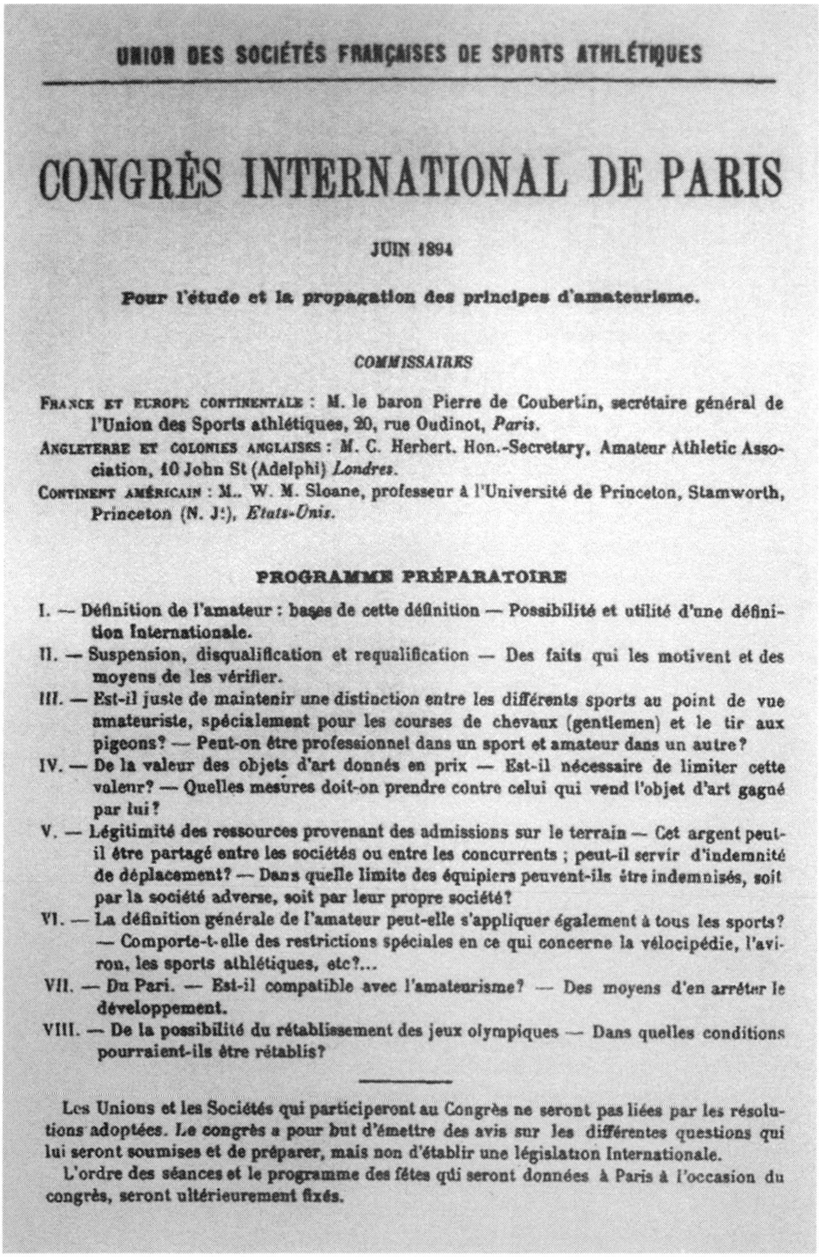

UNION DES SOCIÉTÉS FRANÇAISES DE SPORTS ATHLÉTIQUES

# CONGRÈS INTERNATIONAL DE PARIS

JUIN 1894

**Pour l'étude et la propagation des principes d'amateurisme.**

*COMMISSAIRES*

FRANCE ET EUROPE CONTINENTALE : M. le baron Pierre de Coubertin, secrétaire général de l'Union des Sports athlétiques, 20, rue Oudinot, *Paris*.

ANGLETERRE ET COLONIES ANGLAISES : M. C. Herbert. Hon.-Secretary, Amateur Athletic Association, 10 John St (Adelphi) *Londres*.

CONTINENT AMÉRICAIN : M.. W. M. Sloane, professeur à l'Université de Princeton, Stamworth, Princeton (N. J.), *Etats-Unis*.

**PROGRAMME PRÉPARATOIRE**

I. — Définition de l'amateur : bases de cette définition — Possibilité et utilité d'une définition Internationale.

II. — Suspension, disqualification et requalification — Des faits qui les motivent et des moyens de les vérifier.

III. — Est-il juste de maintenir une distinction entre les différents sports au point de vue amateuriste, spécialement pour les courses de chevaux (gentlemen) et le tir aux pigeons? — Peut-on être professionnel dans un sport et amateur dans un autre?

IV. — De la valeur des objets d'art donnés en prix — Est-il nécessaire de limiter cette valeur? — Quelles mesures doit-on prendre contre celui qui vend l'objet d'art gagné par lui?

V. — Légitimité des ressources provenant des admissions sur le terrain — Cet argent peut-il être partagé entre les sociétés ou entre les concurrents ; peut-il servir d'indemnité de déplacement? — Dans quelle limite des équipiers peuvent-ils être indemnisés, soit par la société adverse, soit par leur propre société?

VI. — La définition générale de l'amateur peut-elle s'appliquer également à tous les sports? — Comporte-t-elle des restrictions spéciales en ce qui concerne la vélocipédie, l'aviron, les sports athlétiques, etc?...

VII. — Du Pari. — Est-il compatible avec l'amateurisme? — Des moyens d'en arrêter le développement.

VIII. — De la possibilité du rétablissement des jeux olympiques — Dans quelles conditions pourraient-ils être rétablis?

Les Unions et les Sociétés qui participeront au Congrès ne seront pas liées par les résolutions adoptées. Le congrès a pour but d'émettre des avis sur les différentes questions qui lui seront soumises et de préparer, mais non d'établir une législation Internationale.

L'ordre des séances et le programme des fêtes qui seront données à Paris à l'occasion du congrès, seront ultérieurement fixés.

Figure 43 - The invitation for the International Congress in Paris, 1894.

did start competing in the games held in Paris, France in 1900. Women from the United States of America and Great Britain were the only women competitors at this time, and they competed in women's golf and tennis matches.

Every four years the Olympic Games are held in a different city around the world. The official opening starts with the lighting of the Olympic torch in a ceremony held in the sacred grove of Altis on the ancient site of Olympia. It is then carried by a runner to an area about a mile away, on the grounds of the current Olympic Academy; here, another flame is lighted at a monument honoring Baron Pierre de Coubertin. A plaque on Coubertin's monument reads,

*"Here rests the heart of the Baron Pierre de Coubertin."*

Once this is done runners relay the torch to the stadium in the city where the games will be held. The flame has become a symbol of the surviving spirit of the ancient competitions; competitions in which women had a part.

FOOTNOTES: Chapter Nine: The Modern Day Olympic Games: Melpomene and The 1896
          Olympic Games

1.      In an article by Karl Lennartz article, he says he believes there were two different
        women runners, one named Stamata Rivithi, and one named Melpomene. According
        to Athanasios Tarasouleas' book, *"Olimpiaka Dromena: Athens 1895-1896*, Stamata and
        Melpomene are the same person and that possibly Stamata was given this name after
        the Greek muse of tragedy.

2.      The race commemorates the run of Pheidippides, an Athenian soldier. Pheidippides,
        in 490 B.C., raced to Athens after the Battle of Marathon and announced the victory
        message: "Rejoice; we conquer!" and then fell dead.

3.      Siamata Rivithi actually finished the race close to the Olympic Stadium at a location
        which is now the Hospital Evagelismos.

4.      P.N.Linardos "From the Vision to the Actions: Demetrios Vikelas" Athens, 1996

# THE MODERN MYTH OF THE FIVE RINGS
# AND THE OLYMPIC GAMES

Five interlocking rings have become the world-wide symbol of the Olympic Games and is commonly accepted as having its roots in antiquity.

David C. Young, in his article, "Myths about the Ancient Games,"[1] dispels the myth of the five rings as a modern day invention having no basis in ancient history.

Young has traced the myth of the rings to two American authors, Lynn and Gray Poole, whose mistaken identification of an old movie prop for an ancient inscription, was perpetuated by numerous unwitting writers copying their work.

The invention of the five rings has its origins from the 1936 Berlin Olympics. The rings were the idea of film-maker, Leni Riefenstahl. Riefenstahl, had them carved into a block of stone for a prop to be used in her film, *Olympia*. The inscribed stone was placed at the stadium at Delphi for a scene with the Olympic torch runner. Here, years later, it was found by Lynn and Gray Poole who believed it to be an authentic inscription from the ancient games at Delphi and published their finding as such. The rest is history.

David Young, in the same article, writes that the Olympic flame is also a myth. However, we did find reference to the ancient flame in Pausanias.

Pausanias describes a hearth with a fire that burns day and night located in the Prytaneum; in ancient Olympia this building was inside the Altis with an exit to the gymnasium. Important people were entertained in a banqueting room, opposite the room with the hearth, within the Prytaneum. This is where they held the feast for the Olympic victors. The ashes from this fire were carried to another alter for "the Olympian god."[2]

Perhaps this is where the Olympic flame, the modern day symbol for peace, derives. Every four years a lighted torch is passed from runner to runner until it arrives in the stadium of the country where the Games are to be held. The passing of the torch is a modern day invention enabling the symbolic flame to be present wherever the games are being held. Of course the passing of the torch was not needed in ancient Greece, when the Olympic Games were always held in the same location, Olympia.

1.   *Archeology* magazine, July/August 1996, page 30.
2.   Paus. BK V.XV.9.

WINNERS
CERTIFICATES

# ARISTOKLEIA

## ELEUTHERIA

Ancient Greek Inscription
(IG IX, II, 526)

### ΑΡΙCΤΟΚΛΕΙΑ ΜΕΓΑΛΟΚΛΕΟΥC ΛΑΡΙCΑΙΑ
### ΣΥΝωΡΙΔΙ ΤΕΛΕΙΑ

Modern Greek Translation

*Ἡ Ἀριστόκλεια, κόρη τοῦ Μεγακλέους, Λαρισαία,
(ἐνίκησε) μέ ἄρμα συρόμενο ἀπό δύο ἄλογα.*

English Translation

*Aristokleia, daughter of Megakles from Larissa, who won
with a chariot drawn by two horses.*

## ΑΒΡΙΣ
## AVRIS

## AMPHIARAIA

Ancient Greek Inscription
(IG VII, 417)

**Ἀβρὶς Καΐκου Κυμαία
κέλητι τελήῳ**

Modern Greek Translation

*Ἡ Ἀβρίς, κόρη τοῦ Καΐκου, ἀπό τήν Κύμη (ἐνίκησε)
μέ ἐνήλικο ἀρσενικό ἄλογο.*

English Translation

*Avris, daughter of Kaikos from Kymi, won in the horserace
with a male horse.*

# ΧΛΩΡΙΣ
# CHLORIS

## HERAEA

Ancient Greek Text
(Paus. Bk.V.XVI.4)

Ἐπανάγουσι δὲ καὶ τῶν παρθένων τὸν ἀγῶνα ἐς τὰ ἀρχαῖα,
Ἱπποδάμειαν τῇ Ἥρᾳ τῶν γάμων τῶν Πέλοπος ἐκτίνουσαν
χάριν τάς τε ἑκκαίδεκα ἀθροῖσαι γυναῖκας λέγοντες καὶ σὺν
αὐταῖς διαθεῖναι πρώτην τὰ Ἡραῖα· μνημονεύουσι δὲ καὶ ὅτι
Χλῶρις νικήσειεν Ἀμφίονος θυγάτηρ μόνη λειφθεῖσα τοῦ
οἴκου.

Modern Greek Translation

Λένε, ὅτι ἡ Ἱπποδάμεια ἐγκαινίασε τά Ἡραῖα...
Καί μνημονεύουν, ὅτι νίκησε ἡ Χλῶρις, θυγατέρα τοῦ Ἀμφίονος...

English Translation

... Hippodamia... arranged the Heraean games for the first
time... Ghloris, daughter of Amphion, was victorious.

## ΔΑΜΟΔΙΚΑ
## DAMODIKA

### (GAME UNKNOWN)

Ancient Greek Inscription
(BCH 1927, pg. 387)

Δαμοδίκα Κρ[άτητος, γυν]ὴ δέ
Ἑρμογένους τ[ο]ῦ Ἀσκληπιάδου
χαῖρε.
[Οὔ]νομα Δαμοδίκα, πόσις ἀγλαὸς Ἑρμογένης μο[ι]
[τί?]μιος ὁ σπείρας δ' ἐμ βιοτᾷ με Κράτης·
[θν]άσκω δ' οὐκ ἀβό[α]τος, ἐπεὶ καὶ παῖδα λέλοιπ[α]
[κα]ὶ κλέος ἐγ νίκας ἅρματι κυδαλίμ[ῳ]·
[ἄ]νερα δ' οὐχ ἰδόμαν ὅτ' ἀπέπνεον, ἀλλ' ἐνὶ Ῥώ[μα]
[πρ]εσβεύων πυμάτων οὐκ ἐνέπλησε χάρι[ν].

Modern Greek Translation

*Δαμοδίκα, κόρη τοῦ Κράτητος
καί γυναῖκα τοῦ Ἑρμογένους τοῦ Ἀσκληπιάδου χαῖρε.
Τό ὄνομά μου εἶναι Δαμοδίκα. Ἐπιφανής
σύζυγός μου ὁ τίμιος Ἑρμογένης καί Κράτης αὐτός πού μ' ἔφερε στή ζωή. Δέν πε-
θαίνω ἄκλαφτη ἀφοῦ καί παιδί ἄφησα καί δόξα ἀπό τήν νίκη μου μέ ἅρμα φημισμέ-
νο. Τόν ἄνδρα μου δέν εἶδα ὅταν ξεψυχοῦσα ἐπειδή ἦταν στή Ρώμη σέ ἀποστολή καί
δέν μοῦ ἔγινε αὐτή ἡ τελευταία χάρη.*

English Translation

Damodika, daughter of Kratis and wife of Hermogenes Asklepiades.  My name is
Damodika, my honorable husband is Hermogenis and my father is Kratis. On my
death, I leave behind my son and the glory from my victory with a glorious chariot. On
my death my husband was in Rome, so I missed the case to see him for the last time.

# ΔΙΟΝΥΣΙΑ
## DIONYSIA

## ISTHMIAN GAMES
## ASKLEPEIAN FESTIVAL

Ancient Greek Inscription
(SIG Inscription #802)

**Διονυσίαν νεικ[ήσασαν Ἴσθμια?] | ἐπὶ ἀγωνοθέτου Ἀντ[ιγόν]ου², | καὶ Ἀσκλάπεια ἐν Ἐπιδαύρῳ | τῇ ἱερᾷ ἐπὶ ἀγων[ο]θέτου Νεικο[τέλου¹⁰ στάδιον, |**

Modern Greek Translation

*Ἡ Διονυσία ἐνίκησε στά Ἴσθμια, ἐπί ἀγωνοθέτου Ἀντιγόνου καί στά Ἀσκληπίεια, στήν ἱερά Ἐπίδαυρο, ἐπί ἀγωνοθέτου Νεικοτέλους σέ ἀγῶνα δρόμου.*

English Translation

*Dionysia won in Isthmia when Antigonos was the organizer of the games, and won in the footrace at the Asklepeia in sacred Epidavros when Nikoteles was the organizer of the games.*

## ϹΥΚΡΑΤϹΙΑ
## EUKRATEIA


## PANATHENAEA


Ancient Greek Inscription
(IG II, Part II, 2314)

**Εὐκράτεια Πολυκράτους [Ἀργεία]
ἄρματι τελ[είῳ].**


Modern Greek Translation

*Ἡ Εὐκράτεια, κόρη τοῦ Πολυκράτους ἀπό τό Ἄργος, (ἐνίκησε) μέ
ἄρμα συρόμενο ἀπό τέσσερα ἄλογα.*


English Translation

*Eukrateia, from Argos and daughter of Polykrates, won in the race with
chariots drawn by four horses.*

# EUKLEIA

## THEOPHANIA?

Ancient Greek Inscription
(BCH 1935, pg. 460)

**[ἅρματι] πωλικῷ Εὔκληια Μη[–]**

Modern Greek Translation

*Ἡ Εὔκλεια νίκησε σέ ἁρματοδρομία μέ πουλάρια.*

English Translation

*Eukleia won in the chariot race with colts.*

# EURYLEONIS

## OLYMPIC GAMES

Ancient Greek Text
(Pausanias BK III, XVII, 6)

**"Πρός δέ τῷ Σκηνώματι ὀνομαζομένῳ γυναικός ἐστιν εἰκών, Λακεδαιμόνιοι δέ Εὐρυλεωνίδα λέγουσιν εἶναι, νίκην δέ ἵππων συνωρίδι ἐνείλετο Ὀλυμπικήν.**

Modern Greek Translation

*... οἱ δέ Λακεδαιμόνιοι λέγουν ὅτι εἶναι ἡ Εὐρυλεωνίς, ἡ ὁποία κατέκτησε Ὀλυμπιακή νίκη μέ ἅρμα συρόμενο ἀπό δύο ἄλογα.*

English Translation

*... Euryleonis, who won an Olympic victory with a two-horse chariot.*

## HEDEA

## ISTHMIAN GAMES
## NEMEAN GAMES

Ancient Greek Inscription
(SIG inscription #802)

**Ἡδέαν νεικήσασαν Ἴσθμια ἐπὶ ἀγωνολθέτου Κορνηλίου Πούλχρου⁶ ἐνόπλιλον⁷ ἄρματι, καὶ Νέμεα στάδιον ἐπὶ ἀγωλνοθέτου Ἀντιγόνου.**

Modern Greek Translation

*Ἡ Ἡδέα, ἐνίκησε στά Ἴσθμια, ἐπὶ ἀγωνοθέτου Κορνηλίου Πούλχρου, μέ πολεμικό ἄρμα ὁπλισμένο· καί στά Νέμεα, ἐπί ἀγωνοθέτου Ἀντιγόνου, σέ ἀγῶνα δρόμου.*

English Translation

*Hedea won the race for war chariots in armor at the Isthmian Games when Cornelius Pulcher was the organizer of the games, and the footrace at the Nemean Games when Antigonos was the organizer of the games...*

# ϹΡΜΙΟΝΗ
# HERMIONE

## PANATHENAEA

Ancient Greek Inscription
(IG II, Part II, 2314)

**[Ἑρμιό]νη [Πολυ]κράτους [Ἀργεία].**

Modern Greek Translation

*Ἡ Ἑρμιόνη, κόρη τοῦ Πολυκράτους ἀπό τό Ἄργος
(ἄγνωστο τό ἀγώνισμα, πιθανότατα ἱπποδρομία).*

English Translation

*Hermione, from Argos and daughter of Polykrates, won in the…*
(contest unknown but probably a horserace).

# ΗΠΙΟΝΗ
## IPIONI

## ELEUTHERIA

Ancient Greek Inscription
(Review de philologie # 35)

**[Ἠ]π??ιόνη {[Ἀλ]κ?ι?όνη?} Πολυξένου Θεσσαλή ἀπό Λα?ρίσης τῆς [Πελασγίδος].**

Modern Greek Translation

*Ἡ Ἠπιόνη, κόρη τοῦ Πολυξένου, ἀπό τήν Λάρισα τῆς Θεσσαλίας.*

English Translation

*Ipione, daughter of Polyxenos, from Larissa in Thessaly.*

# ΚΑΣΙΑ ΜΝΑΣΙΘΕΑ
# KASIA MNASITHEA

## OLYMPIC GAMES

Ancient Greek Inscription
(Ol. inscription #233)

**Κασία Μ[νασιθέα, Μ(άρχου) Βετληνοῦ Λαίτου θ[υγάτηρ, νικήσασα] | Ὀλυμπί[α ἄρματι πω]|λικῷ ἐ[πὶ τῆς τ.. Ὀλυμ]- πιάδος, [Διὶ Ὀλυμπίῳ].**

Modern Greek Translation

*Ἡ Κασία Μνασιθέα, κόρη τοῦ Μάρχου Βετληνοῦ Λαίτου, ἐνίκησε στούς Ὀλυμπιακούς Ἀγῶνες μέ ἄρμα συρόμενο ἀπό νεαρά ἄλογα κατά τήν ... Ὀλυμπιάδα, πρός τιμήν τοῦ Ὀλυμπίου Διός.*

English Translation

*Kasia Mnasithea, daughter of Marcus Vetlenus Laetus, was victorious at the Olympic Games in the chariot race with colts.*

# ΚΥΝΙΣΚΑ
# KYNISKA

## OLYMPIC GAMES

Ancient Greek Inscription
(AE, inscription #160)

**Σπάρτας μὲν [βασιλῆες ἐμοὶ] Ιπατέρες καὶ ἀδελφοί,
ἅ!ρματι δ' ὠκυπόδων ἵππων] [νικῶσα Κυνίσκα
εἰκόνα τάνδ' ἔστασε· μόν[αν] [δ' ἐμέ φαμι γυναικῶν
Ἑλλάδος ἐκ πάσας τό[ν]Ιδε λαβεῖν στέφανον.
Ἀπελλίας Καλλικλέος ἐπόησε.**

Modern Greek Translation

*Οἱ γονεῖς μου καί τά ἀδέλφια μου (εἶναι) βασιλεῖς τῆς Σπάρτης.
Ἐγώ, ἡ Κυνίσκα, ἐνίκησα στήν ἀρματοδρομία μέ γοργοπόδαρα ἄλογα. Ἔστησα αὐτό τό ἄγαλμα καί λέω πώς εἶμαι ἡ μόνη γυναῖκα ἀπό
ὅλη τήν Ἑλλάδα, πού κέρδισα αὐτό τό στεφάνι. Ὁ γλύπτης Ἀπελλῆς,
ὁ υἱός τοῦ Καλλικλῆ, ἐποίησε.*

English Translation

*My fathers and brothers (are) the Kings of Sparta. I, Kyniska, won in
the chariot race with swift-footed horses. I erect this statue and I say that
I am the only woman from all of Greece who has ever won this crown.
Made by Appeleas, son of Kallikles.*

# ΛΥΣΙS
# LYSIS

## AMPHIARAIA

Ancient Greek Inscription
(AE, inscription #140)

**Λυ]σὶ[ς] Ἐ[ϱ]μώνακτος Μάγνησσα ἀπὸ Μαιάνδρου·
κέλητι πωλικῷ**

Modern Greek Translation

*Ἡ Λυσίς, κόρη τοῦ Ἑρμώνακτος, ἀπό τήν Μαγνησία,
ἀπό τόν Μαίανδρο, (ἐνίκησε) μέ νεαρό ἀρσενικό ἄλογο.*

English Translation

*Lysis, a woman from Magnesia and daughter of Ermonax,
won in the race with a colt.*

# ΜΝΑΣΙΜΑΧΑ
## ΜΝΑSIΜΑΗΑ

## AMPHIARAIA

Ancient Greek Inscription
(AE, inscription #142)

**ἅρματι πωλικῷ Μ]νασιμάχα Φοξίνου Θεσσαλὴ ἀπὸ Κρανῶννος**

Modern Greek Translation

*Ἡ Μνασιμάχα, κόρη τοῦ Φοξίνου, Θεσσαλή, ἀπό τήν Κρανῶννα, (ἐνίκησε) μέ ἅρμα συρόμενο ἀπό νεαρά ἄλογα.*

English Translation

*Mnasimaha, daughter of Foxinos from Kranon in Thessaly, won in the chariot race with colts.*

# ΜΝΑΕΙΑΔΑ
# MNASIATHA

## PANATHENAEA

Ancient Greek Inscription
(IG II, Part II, 2314)

**[....... Μνασι]άδα Ἀργεία ἀπ' Ἀχαιΐας
[ἅ]ρματι πωλικῷ**

Modern Greek Translation

*Ἡ Μνασιάδα ἀπό τό Ἄργος, ἀπό τήν Ἀχαΐα, (ἐνίκησε)
μέ ἅρμα συρόμενο ἀπό νεαρά ἄλογα.*

English Translation

*Mnasiatha from Argos in Achaiia won in the chariot race with colts.*

# ΝΙΚΗΓΟΡΑ
# NIKIGORA

## (GAME UNKNOWN)

### Ancient Greek Text
(Paus. manuscript 1410 margin)

**Νικηγόραν Νικόφιλος νικήσασαν δρόμῳ τὸν τῶν παρθένων δρόμον τῇδ' ἀνέθηκα λίθου Παρίου τὴν γλυκυτάτην ἀδελφήν**

### Modern Greek Translation

*Ἐγώ, ὁ Νικόφιλος, ἔστησα αὐτό τό ἄγαλμα ἀπό Παριανό μάρμαρο, γιά τήν ἀγαπημένη μου ἀδελφή Νικηγόρα, πού νίκησε στούς ἀγῶνες δρόμου τῶν κοριτσιῶν.*

### English Translation

*I, Nikophilos, erected this statue of Parian marble to my beloved sister, Nikigora, victor in the girls' race.*

# ΘΕΟΔΟΤΑ ΑΝΤΙΦΑΝΟΥΣ
# THEODOTA ANTIPHANUS

## OLYMPIC GAMES

Ancient Greek Inscription
(Ol. inscription #203)

**Θεοδότα Ἀντιφάνους Ἠλεία] Ὀλύμπια ἅρματι πωλικῷ.**

Modern Greek Translation

Ἡ Θεοδότα, κόρη τοῦ Ἀντιφάνους, ἀπό τήν Ἤλιδα, (ἐνίκησε) στούς
Ὀλυμπιακούς Ἀγῶνες μέ ἅρμα συρόμενο ἀπό νεαρά ἄλογα.

English Translation

*Theodota, daughter of Antiphanos, from Elis,*
*won in the chariot race with colts.*

# ΤΙΜΑΡΕΤΑ
# TIMARETA

## OLYMPIC GAMES

Ancient Greek Inscription
(Ol. inscription #201)

**Τιμαρέτα Φιλίστου Ἠλεία | Ὀλύμπια συνωρίδι τελείᾳ.**

Modern Greek Translation

*Ἡ Τιμαρέτα, κόρη τοῦ Φιλίστου, ἀπό τήν Ἤλιδα, (ἐνίκησε)
στούς Ὀλυμπιακούς Ἀγῶνες μέ ἅρμα συρόμενο ἀπό δύο ἄλογα.*

English Translation

*Timareta from Elis, daughter of Philistos, won with a chariot drawn by
two horses.*

# ΤΡΥΦΩΣΑ
# TRYPHOSA

## PYTHIAN GAMES
## ISTHMIAN GAMES

Ancient Greek Inscription
(SIG Inscription #802)

⁵ **Τρυφῶσαν νεικήσασαν Πύθια ἐlπὶ ἀγωνοθετῶν Ἀντιγόνου² | καὶ Κλεομαχίδα³, καὶ Ἴσθμια⁴ ἐπὶ ἀγωνοθέτου Ἰουβεντίου Πρόlκλου, στάδιον κατὰ τὸ ἑξῆς, πρώτη παρθένων⁵, |**

Modern Greek Translation

Ἡ Τρυφῶσα ἐνίκησε στά Πύθια, ἐπί ἀγωνοθετῶν Ἀντιγόνου καί Κλεομαχίδα, καί στά Ἴσθμια ἐπί ἀγωνοθέτου Ἰουβεντίου Πρόκλου, σέ ἀγῶνα δρόμου, πρώτη ἀπό τίς παρθένους.

English Translation

*Tryphosa won the footrace at the Pythian Games when Antigonos and Kleomachidas were the organizers of the games, and the footrace at the ensuing Isthmian Games when Iouventios Proklos was the organizer of the games, (Tryphosa was) the first of the virgins.*

# ΒΙΛΙΣΤΙΧΗ
# VELESTEHE

## OLYMPIC GAMES

Ancient Greek Text
First Victory
(Oxyrhynchus papyrus #2082, fragment 6)

**[Βιλιστιχης Μ]ακετιδος πωλικ[ο]ν
[τεθριππον] αυτη Πτολεμα[ιου
[Φιλαδελφου ετ]αι[ρ]α εστιν [**

Modern Greek Translation

*Ή Βιλιστίχη ἀπό τήν Μακεδονία (ἐνίκησε) μέ ἄρμα
συρόμενο ἀπό τέσσερα νεαρά ἄλογα. Αὐτή εἶναι
ἡ ἐρωμένη τοῦ Πτολεμαίου Φιλαδέλφου.*

English Translation

*Velestehe, a woman from Macedonia, won in the four-colt chariot.
She is the mistress of Ptolemy II Philadelphos.*

# ΒΕΛΙΣΤΙΧΗ
## VELESTEHE

## OLYMPIC GAMES

Ancient Greek Text
Second Victory
(Pausanias, Bk V.VIII.11)

[συν]έθεσαν δὲ ὕστερον καὶ συνωρίδα πώλων καὶ πῶλον κέλητα·
ἐπὶ μὲν δὴ τῇ συνωρίδι Βελιστίχην ἐκ Μακεδονίας τῆς ἐπὶ
θαλάσσῃ γυναῖκα.

Modern Greek Translation

… Ὀργάνωσαν ἀγῶνες μέ ἅρματα συρόμενα ἀπό ζεύγη νεαρῶν
ἀρσενικῶν ἀλόγων… (καί) μία γυναίκα, ἡ Βελιστίχη, ἀπό τήν
παραθαλάσσια Μακεδονία, ἀνακηρύχθηκε νικήτρια…

English Translation

… they instantied races between chariots drawn by pairs of foals…
(and) a woman Velestehe, from the coast of Macedonia, was proclaimed
victor…

# ΒΕΡΕΝΙΚΗ
# VERENIKE

## NEMEAN GAMES

Modern Greek Translation

*Ἔχω ἕνα νικητήριο τραγούδι νά τραγουδήσω, γιατί μόλις
ἔφθασαν ἀπό τό Ἄργος στήν Αἴγυπτο, τά νέα, πώς στήν Νεμέα,
στήν ἀρματοδρομία, τά ἄλογά σου ἐνίκησαν...*

English Translation

*I have a song of victory to sing: for news has just come from Argos
to Egypt, that at Nemea, in the chariot race, your horses won...*

**ΖΕΥΞΩ**
**(Κόρη τοῦ Ἀρίστωνος)**
**ZEUXO**
**(Daughter of Ariston)**

**PANATHENAEA**

Ancient Greek Inscription
(IG II, Part II, 2313)

**Ζευξὼ Ἀρίστωνος Κυρηναία**
**ἅρματι τελείῳ**

Modern Greek Translation

*Ἡ Ζευξώ, κόρη τοῦ Ἀρίστωνος, Κυρηναία, (ἐνίκησε)*
*μέ ἅρμα συρόμενο ἀπό τέσσερα ἄλογα.*

English Translation

*Zeuxo, from Kyrene and daughter of Ariston, won in the race*
*with chariots drawn by four horses.*

## ΖΕΥΞΩ
## (Κόρη τοῦ Πολυκράτους)
## ZEUXO
## (Daughter of Polykrates)

## PANATHENAEA

Ancient Greek Inscription
(IG II, Part 2, 2314)

**[Ζευξώ Πολυκρ]άτου Ἀργεία ἀπ' Ἀχαΐας
[κέ]λητι τελείῳ**

Modern Greek Translation

*Ἡ Ζευξώ, κόρη τοῦ Πολυκράτους, ἀπό τό Ἄργος ἀπό τήν Ἀχαΐα,
(ἐνίκησε) μέ ἐνήλικο ἀρσενικό ἄλογο.*

English Translation

*Zeuxo, from Argos in Achaiia and daughter of Polykrates, won in the
horserace with a male horse.*

# ΑΓΝΩΣΤΟ ΟΝΟΜΑ
## MISSING NAME

## PANATHENAEA

Ancient Greek Inscription
(IG II, Part II, 2314)

.............. Ἀργεία ἀπ' Ἀχαΐας
[ἅρματι τ]ελείῳ.

Modern Greek Translation

*... ἀπό τό Ἄργος, ἀπό τήν Ἀχαΐα , (ἐνίκησε) μέ ἅρμα συρόμενο ἀπό τέσσερα ἄλογα.*

English Translation

*... a woman from Argos in Achaiia, won in the race with chariots drawn by four horses.*

# BIBLIOGRAPHY

*Akropolis* (Athens.) 29 March and 31 March 1896.

Alexiou, Stylianos, Nikolas Platon, and Hanni Guaella. *Ancient Crete.* NewYork: Praeger, 1968.

*Ancient Athletics of the Ancient World.* Chicago, IL: Ares Publishers, 1983.

Anderson, J.K., trans. *Ancient Greek Horsemanship.* Berkeley, CA: University of California Press, 1961. See no. 885. With a translation of Xenophon's Perihippikes, 1520.

Arafat, K.W. *Pausanias' Greece: Ancient Artists and Roman Rulers.* Cambridge, MA: Cambridge University Press, 1996.

"Archeology in Greece." *Archeological Reports for 1976-1977.*

"Archeology in Greece." *Archeological Reports for 1982-1983.*

*Archeologiki Ephimeris.* Athens: 1925–1926. Amphiariou inscriptions.

*Archeologikon Deltion.* Volume 10. Athens: 1926.

Aristophanes. *Lysistrata.* New York: Panurge Press.

Arrigoni, Giampieia, ed. *Le Donne In Greci.* Italy: Gius, Laterza and Figli, 1985.

*Asty* (Athens.) 30 March and 12 April 1896.

Athanassakis, Apostolos N. *The Homeric Hymns.* Baltimore: Johns Hopkins University Press, 1976.

Athenaeos. *The Deipnosophists.* Translated by Charles Burton Gulick. Cambridge, Mass: Harvard University Press, 1970.*Atti Della Accademia Nazionale Dei Lincei.* Volume VIII. Rome: 1959.

Attridge, Harold W., and Gohei Hata, eds. *Eusebius, Christianity and Judaism.* Detroit: Wayne State University Press, 1992.

Avery, Catherine B., ed. *The New Century Classical Dictionary.* Appleton-Cetury-Crofts, 1962.

Babbitt, F.C. "Plutarch." Loeb Classical Library. Harvard University Press, 1968.

Banks, J., trans. *The Idylls of Theocritus, bion, and Moschus, and the War Songs of Tyrtaeus.* London: Bell and Dadly, 1873.

Bell, Robert E. *Women of Classical Mythology.* Oxford: University Press, 1991.

Boardman, J., and O. Murray. *The Oxford History of the Classical World.* Oxford: Oxford University Press, 1986.

Bradford, A.S. "Gynaikokratoumemoi: Did Spartan Woman Rule
   Spartan Men?" *The Ancient World.* ns 4:1 and 14:2.
Burkert, Walter. *Greek Religion: Archaic and Classical.* Translated by
   John Raffan. Oxford: Basil Blackwell Publisher, 1985.
Butler, H.E., trans. *Propertius.* Harvard University Press, 1962.
Carroll, Mitchell. *Greek Women.* Philadelphia: Rittenhouse, 1907.
Catling, H.W. *The Council of the Society for the Promotion of Hellenic Studies and the*
   *Managing Committee of the British School at Athens,* 1983.
Chimes, K.M.T. *Ancient Sparta.* Greenwood Press, 1971.Cornford, F.M.
   *The Origin of the Olympic Games* (Temis, 1912). Edited by
   J.E. Harrison. Cambridge: University Press, 1962, pp. 212-259.
Cottrell, Leonard, ed. *The Past: A Concise Encyclopedia of Archeology.*
   New York: Hawthorn, 1960.
Curtius, Ernst. *The History of Greece.* Translated by Adolphus William
   Ward. New York: Scribner.
*Dictionary.* Third edition. Oxford: Oxford University Press, 1996.
Dittenbergero, Guilelmo. *Sylloge Inscriptionum Graecarum.* Lipsiae: Apud
   S. Hirzelium, 1917. Volumen Alterum.
Drees, Ludwig. *Olympia Gods, Artists, and Athletes.* New York: Frederick
   A.   Praeger, 1968.
Dryden and Clough, trans. *Plutarch's Lives of Illustrious Men.*
   Philadelphia: John C. Winston, 1908.
Du Buit, O.P. *Biblical Archeology.* New York: Hawthorne, 1960.
Edmonds, J.M., trans. *Lyra Graeca.* Cambridge, Mass: Harvard University
   Press, 1963. Volume I.
Edwards, I.E.S., C.J. Gadd, and N.G.I. Hammond, eds. *The Cambridge*
   *Ancient History.* Cambridge: University Press, 1970.
Eisen, G. "Sports and Women in Antiquity." Thesis, Amherst, 1976.
*Encyclopedia 1993-1997.* Microsoft Encarta 98.
Estia (Athens). 23 March 1896.
Euripides. *Andromache.* Translated by David Kovacs. Loeb Classical
   Library. Harvard University Press, 1995.
Eusebius. *Christianity and Judaism.* Edited by Harold W. Attridge and
   Gohei Hata. Detroit: Wayne State University Press, 1992.
Fairbanks, Arthur, trans. *Philostratus Images.* The Loeb Classical Library.
   Cambridge, Mass: Harvard University Press, 1931.
Farnell, Lewis Richard. *The Cult of the Greek States.* Chicago: Aegean
   Press Inc., 1971.

Finley, John H., Jr. *Pindar and Aeschylus*. Cambridge, Mass: Harvard
University Press, 1955.

French, E.B. "Archeology in Greece." *Archeological Reports for
1989-1990*.

Gardiner, Norman E. *Olympia: Its History and Remains*. Oxford:
Clarendon Press, 1925.

Godolphin, Francis R.B., ed. *The Greek Historians*. 2 vols. New York:
Random House Publishers, 1942.

*Greece, Sports and Culture*. Athens: Ministry of Culture, General
Secretariat of Sports 1988.

Harlan, Hugh. *History of Olympic Games: Ancient and Modern*.
Los Angeles: Bureau of Athletic Research, 1932.

Harris, Cyril M., ed. *Illustrated Dictionary of Historic Architecture*. Dover
Publications, 1977.

Harris, H.A. *Greek Athletes and Athletics*. London: Hutchinson, 1964.

Holmberg, Erik J. *Delphi and Olympia*. Gothenburg, Sweden: Paul Astrom
Publisher, 1979.

Hornblower, Simon and Anthony Spawfoth, eds. *The Oxford Classical*

Howell, Reet, ed. *Leisure, Her Story in Sport*. 1982.

Hunt, Arthur S., ed. and trans. *The Oxyrhynchus Papyri*. Part XVII.
London:Egypt Exploration Society, 1927.

*Inscriptiones Graecae*. Consilio Et Auctoritate, Academiae Litterarum
Regiae Borussicae editae. Vol. II, Part II. Berolini Apud
Georgium Reimerum, MDCCCLXXXIII.

*Inscriptiones Graecae:Laconiae Messeniac Arcadiac*. Edited by
Gualtherus Kolbe. Vol. V. 1913.

*International Olympic Academy: Thirtieth Session 20 June-5 July 1990*.
International Olympic Committee in Collaboration with the International Olympic Academy. 1990.

Jeffreys, Elizabeth, Michael Jeffreys, and Roger Scott, trans. *The
Chronicle of John Malalas*. Melbourne: Australian Association
for Byzantine Studies, 1986.

Jowett, Benjamin, trans. *History, Thukydides*. Twayne Publishing, 1963.

Kaldis-Henderson, Nota. "A Study of Women in Ancient Elis." Ph.D.
diss., University of Minnesota, Loyola University, 1979.

Kenna,V.E.G., "Seals,"*Cretan Seals*. Oxford: Clarendon Press, 1960.

Kieran, John and Arthur Daley. *The Story of the Olympic Games: 776 BC to 1972*. New York: J.B. Lippincott Company, 1973.

Kirkwood, G.M. *Poetry and Poetics from Ancient Greece to the Renaissance*. Ithaca: Cornell University Press, 1975.

Kokkinou, Sophia. *Greek Mythology*. Athens: Intercarta, 1989.

Koutoulas, Thiamandis. "Heraea: The Unknown Olympic Games for Women in Ancient Greece." *Thavlos, issue 148, April, 1944*.

Lattimore, Richmond, trans. *The Odes of Pindar*. Chicago: University of Chicago Press, 1976.

Lee, Hugh M. "Stadia and Starting Gates," *Archeology*. Jul/Aug. 1996.

Lefkowitz, Mary R. and Maureen B. Fant. *Women's Life in Greece and Rome*. 1982.

Leigh. *Coubertin: 1912 Essay*. 1974.

Lempriere, John. *Bibliotheca Classica: or a Classical Dictionary*. New York and London: Garland Publishing, Inc., 1984.

Levi, Peter, trans. *Pausanias Guide to Greece*. Middlesex: Penguin, 1971.

*Lexikon Icono-Graphicum Mytho-Logiae Classicae*. Artemis. Vol. II.

Linardos, P.N. *From the Vision to the Action: Demetrios Vikelas*. Athens, 1996.

Logiadou–Platonos, S. and Nanno Marinatos. *Crete*. Athens.

*Los Angeles Times Book of the 1984 Olympics, The*. Los Angeles: Los Angeles, 1984.

MacAloon, John J. *This Great Symbol*. Chicago: The University of Chicago Press, 1981.

MacDonald, Francis, trans. *The Republic of Plato*. Oxford University Press, 1975.

Malalas, Joannes. "Chronographia," *Corpus Scriptorum Historiae Byzantinae*. Edited by B.G. Nieburhrii. Athens: Haralambos Spanos Publication.

Mandell, Richard d. *The First Modern Olympics*. Berkeley: University of California Press, 1906.

Marchant, E.C., trans. *Xenophon, Memorabilia and Oeconomicus*. 1923. Cambridge, Mass: Harvard University Press, 1959.

*Message D'Athenes*. (France) 02 March 1896.

Miller, Donna Mae. "Images of Ancient Greek Sportswomen in the Novels of Mary Renault." *Arete: The Journal of sports Literature*. San Diego: San Diego University Press, Fall 1985.

Miller, Stephen G. *Arete: Ancient Writers, Papyri, and Inscriptions on the Ideals of Greek Athletics and Games.* Chicago: Ares, 1979.

–. *Arete: Greek Sports from Ancient Sources.* Berkeley: University of California Press, 1991.

–. "The Theorodokoi of the Nemean Games." *Hisperia*, Apr/Jun, 1988.

–. "Tunnel Vision: the Nemean Games." *Archeology*, Jan/Feb, 1980. Vol. 33, number 1.

*Mind and Body: Athletic contests in Ancient Greece.* Athens: Ministry of Culture and the National Hellenic Committee, I.C.O.M.

Montgomery, H.C. *The Controversy About the Origins of the Olympic Games.* 1936.

Moretti, Luigi. *Inscriptiones Graecae Urbis Romae.* Rome: Studi Pubblicati Dall' Istituto Italiano per la Storia Antica, 1929.

–. *Iscrizioni Agonistiche Greche.* Edited by Angelo Signorelli. fasc. 12. Rome: Studi Pubblicati Dall' Istituto Italiano per la Storia Antica, 1953.

Morgan, Catherine. *Athletes and Oracles.* Cambridge University Press.

Mosshammer, Alden A. *The Chronicle of Eusebius and Greek Chronographic Tradition.* Lewisburg: Bucknell University Press, 1979.

Nilsson, Martin P. *Minoan-Mycenean Religion and Its Survival in Greek Religion.* New York: Biblo and Tannen, 1971.

Norman, E. and M.A. Gardiner. *Greek Athletic Sports and Festivals.* London: Macmillan, 1910.

North, Sir Thomas, trans. *Plutarch's Lives.* London: Bell and Daldy, 1873.

*Notes on Some Points in Xenophon's* Peri Hippikes. 1960.

*Olympic Games in Ancient Greece, The.* Athens: Ekdotike, 1976.

Palaeologos, Kl. "Running." *The Olympic Games in Ancient Greece,* Athens: Ekdotike Publisher, 1982.

Palmer–Sikelianos, Eva. *Upward Panic: The Autobiography of Eva Palmer-Sikelianos.* New York: Harwood, 1993.

Panaiotou, Niki D. *Delphi: Past and Present.* Athens: Gnosis, 1993.

Papahatzis, Nicos. *Ancient Corinth: The Museum of Corinth, Isthmia and Sicyon.* Athens: Ekdotike, 1996.

–. *Ancient Corinth.* Athens: Ekodotike, 1996.

Parke, H.W. *Festivals of the Athenians.* London: Thames and Hudson, 1977.

Paul, C. Robert and Jack Orr. *The Olympic Games: The Thrills and Drama from Ancient Greece to the Present.* New York: Lion Press, 1968.

*Paulys Real-Encyclopadie der Classischen Altertumswissenschaft.* Bergonnen von Georg Vissowa. Stuttgart: J.B. Metzlersche Verlagsbuchhandlung, 1923.

Pausanias. *Pausania' Guide to Greece.* Translated by Peter Levi. Middlesex: Penguin, 1971.

–. *Pausanias' Description of Greece.* Translated by J.G. Frazier. 6 Volumes. New York: Biblo and Tannen.

–. *Pausanias'Description of Greece.* Translated by Georgiadis.

–. *Pausanias' Guide to Ancient Greece.* Translated by Christian Habicht. Berkeley: University of California Press, 1985.

Pease, C.A. *The Toils and Travels of Odysseus.* Chapter XV. U.S.A: Allyn and Bacon, 1926. Odysseus Talks with Penelope and is Recognized by Eurycleia.

*Perseus Program.* Tufts University. http://www.perseus.tufts.edu/

Philostratus. *Gymnasticus27.*

Phlegon of Tralles. "Olympic Chronicles." *Scriptores Rerum Mirabilium Graeci.* Edited by Antonius Westermann. London: Brunsvga, 1839.

*Plutarch: The Dryden Translation.* Chicago: William Benton, 1952.

Plutarch. *Plutarch's Lives.* Translated by Bernadotte Perrin. London: William Heinemann, LTD.

Pomeroy, Sarah B. *Goddesses, Whores, Wives, and Slaves.* New York: Schocken, 1975.

Raschke, Wendy J., ed. *The Archeology of the Olympics.* Wisconsin: University of Wisconsin Press, 1998.

Richter, Giesela. *Sculpture and Sculptors of the Greeks.* New Haven: Yale University Press, 1950.

Ringwood, Irene C. "Agonistic Features of Local Greek festivals Chiefly From Inscriptional Evidence." Ph.D. diss., Columbia University, 1927.

Robinson, Rachael Sargent, trans. *Sources for the History of Greek Athletics.* Cincinnati: Self-published, 1975.

Romano, David G. "The Ancient Stadium: Athletes and Arete." *The Ancient World.* ns 8.1 and 8.2.

Ross, Mark. "Reviving Nemea's Games." *Archeology*, Jul/Aug, 1996.

Rutgers, I., ed. "A List of Olympic Victors." *Sextius Julius Africanus*. Chicago: Ares Publications.

Sandys, Sir John. *The Odes of Pindar*. Cambridge, Mass: Harvard University Press, 1961.

Sargent, Thelma, trans. *The Idyllis of Theocritus*. New York: Norton, 1982.

Saunders, Trevor J. *Plato: The Laws*. London: Penguin Books, 1970.

Scanlon, T.F. "Games for Girls." *Archeology*, Jul/Aug, 1996.

–. *Greek and Roman Athletics: A Bibliography*. Chicago: Ares, 1984.

Scanlon, T.F., trans. *Sport and Recreation in Ancient Greece: A Sourcebook*.

Segrave, J. and D. Chu, eds. "Human Kinetics." *Olympism*, Champaign, Ill.1981.

Seltman, Charles. *Women in Antiquity*. New York: St. Martin's Press, 1955.

Seyffert, Oskar. *Dictionary of Classical Antiquities*. Cleveland and New York: Meridian Books. The World Publishing Company, 1963.

Simon, Erica. *Festivals of Athens*. Madison: The University of Wisconsin Press, 1983.

Smith, Sir William. *Smaller Classical Dictionary*. Revised by E.H. Blakeney And John Warrington. Dutton and Company, Inc.

Smith, William Benjamin and Walter Miller, trans. *The Iliad of Homer*. New York: Macmillan, 1945.

Spatz, Lois. *Aristophanes*. Boston: 1978.

*Supplementum Epigraphicum Graecum*. Edited by H.W. Pleket and R.S. Stroud. Amsterdam: J.C. Gieben, 1983 (vol. XXXIII,) 1985 (vol. XXXV,) 1987 (vol. XXXVII,) 1990 (vol. XL,) 1994 (XLIV.)

Tarasouleas, Thanasis. *Olimbiaka Dromena, Athens 1985-1986*. Athens, 1997.

Themelis, Petros G. *Delphi, the Archeological Site and the Museum*. Athens: Ekdotiki.

Thompson, J.G. "Athletics and Gymnastics in Ancient Greece." Ph.D. diss., Penn. State University Press, 1971. 2584a.

Thurston, Harry, ed. *Harper's Dictionary of Classical Literature and Antiquities*. Harper and Peck Brothers Publishers, 1898.

Toomey, Bill and K. Barry. *The Olympic Challenge*. Reston: Reston Publishing, 1984.

Tripp, Edward. *Crowell's Handbook of Classical Mythology.*

Tsountas, Chrestos and J. Irving Manatt. *The Mycenean Age.* Chicago: Argonaut, 1969.

Vaughan, Agnes Carr. *House of the Double Axe.* New York: Doubleday, 1959.

Vernant, Jean Pierre. *The Origins of Greek Thought.* Ithaca: Cornell University Press, 1982.

Von Felix, Jacoby. *Fragmente Der Griechischen Historiker.* Brill: E.J. Leiden, 1962.

Ward, Anne. *Adventures in Archeology.* London: Hamlyn, 1977.

Weigall, Arthur. *Nero, the Singing Emperor of Rome.* New York: G.P. Putnam and Sons, 1930.

Welldon, J.E.C., trans. *The Politics of Aristotle.* New York: Macmillan.

Woodcock, P.G. *Concise Dictionary of Ancient History.* Philosophical Library. New York, 1955.

Woody, Thomas. *Life and Education in Early Societies.* New York: The Macmillan Company, 1959.

Woolum, Janet. *Outstanding Women Athletes.* Oryx Press, 1992.

Wright, F.A. *Feminism in Greek Literature.* Port Washington, New York: Kennikat, 1969.

Wright, Wilmer Cave, trans. *The Letters of Alciphron, Aelian and Philostratus.* The Loeb Classical Library. Cambridge, Mass: Harvard University Press, 1949.

–. *Philostratus and Eunapius, the Lives of the Sophists.* The Loeb Classical Library. Cambridge, Mass: Harvard University Press, 1921.

Yalouris, A. and N. Yalouris. *Olympia: Guide to the Museum and the Sanctuary.* Athens: Ekdotiki, 1995.

Yalouris, Nicolaos. *Ancient Elis, the Cradle of the Olympic Games.* Athens: Adam, 1998.

Yiannaki, Thomas. *Zappies and Sinhrones Olimpiades.* Athens, 1993.

Young, David C. "Myths About the Ancient Games." *Archeology.* Jul/Aug, 1996.

Zinserling, Verena. *Women in Ancient Greece.*

# INDEX AND PRONUNCIATION GUIDE

# U

# V

# W

# X

# Y

# Z

## ABOUT THE AUTHORS

Anne Reese was born in Seattle, Washington. She studied Anthropology at the University of Washington in Seattle. She also studied at the University of the Americas, in Mexico City, and the University of California at Irvine.

Irini Vallera-Rickerson was born in Athens, Greece. She recieved her doctorate in Architecture at the University of Florence, Italy. She is a professor of Art History and Gallery Director at Orange Coast College in Costa Mesa, California, as well as professor of History of Architecture and Furniture at Saddleback College in Mission Viejo, California. Irini lectures at the University of California at Los Angeles, as well as the University of California at Irvine.

In 1994, Irini received the prestigious award of "Teacher of the Year" in Orange County, California.

The authors have a great passion for ancient Greece and have traveled throughout Greece researching ancient Greek women athletes.